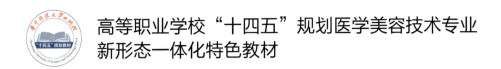

高等职业学校"十四五"规划医学美容技术专业
新形态一体化特色教材

COSMETOLOGY APPLICATION ENGLISH
美容应用英语

主　编　魏丹丹　杨　琴　余芊芊

副主编　邓叶青　李　琳　周　彧　徐　曼

编　者　（按姓氏笔画排序）

邓叶青　广东岭南职业技术学院

刘　颖　江西医学高等专科学校

李　琳　江西中医药高等专科学校

杨　琴　江西中医药高等专科学校

何丽琴　江西中医药高等专科学校

余芊芊　湖北职业技术学院

周　彧　达州中医药职业学院

姚　艳　江西医学高等专科学校

徐　曼　江西医学高等专科学校

崔　宁　廊坊卫生职业学院

魏丹丹　廊坊卫生职业学院

华中科技大学出版社
http://press.hust.edu.cn
中国·武汉

内 容 简 介

本教材为高等职业学校"十四五"规划医学美容技术专业新形态一体化特色教材。

本教材内容共八个单元,包括美容专业概况、美容前台、面部护理、身体护理、彩妆产品和化妆师、美甲、美容行业法律法规及沟通与服务。每个单元分为听、说、读、实用写作四个部分,并包含能力检测和课程思政内容,配备教学 PPT、音频、视频等数字资源,可满足学生深入学习美容英语的要求。

本教材适合高等职业学校医学美容技术、美容美体艺术、人物形象设计等专业使用,也适用于中高级美容师的职业培训,还可作为美容从业人员的职场参考书。

图书在版编目(CIP)数据

美容应用英语 / 魏丹丹,杨琴,余芊芊主编. -- 武汉 : 华中科技大学出版社,2024.7.
ISBN 978-7-5772-1081-0
Ⅰ．F719.9
中国国家版本馆 CIP 数据核字第 2024BU4501 号

美容应用英语
Meirong Yingyong Yingyu

魏丹丹　杨　琴　余芊芊　主编

策划编辑：居　颖	
责任编辑：曾奇峰	
封面设计：金　金	
责任校对：朱　霞	
责任监印：周治超	

出版发行：华中科技大学出版社(中国·武汉)　　电话：(027)81321913
　　　　　武汉市东湖新技术开发区华工科技园　　邮编：430223
录　　排：华中科技大学惠友文印中心
印　　刷：武汉科源印刷设计有限公司
开　　本：787mm×1092mm　1/16
印　　张：10.5
字　　数：301 千字
版　　次：2024 年 7 月第 1 版第 1 次印刷
定　　价：49.80 元

本书若有印装质量问题,请向出版社营销中心调换
全国免费服务热线：400-6679-118　　竭诚为您服务
版权所有　侵权必究

高等职业学校"十四五"规划医学美容技术专业新形态一体化特色教材编委会

主任委员 胡 野
企业顾问 叶秋玲

副主任委员（按姓氏笔画排序）

孙 晶	白城医学高等专科学校	赵 丽	辽宁医药职业学院
杨加峰	宁波卫生职业技术学院	赵自然	吉林大学第一医院
何 伦	中国整形美容协会	蔡成功	沧州医学高等专科学校

委 员（按姓氏笔画排序）

王丕琦	红河卫生职业学院	郑宏来	广西卫生职业技术学院
邓叶青	广东岭南职业技术学院	郑俊清	铁岭卫生职业学院
冯霜雪	海南卫生健康职业学院	赵 红	济南护理职业学院
刘小维	辽宁何氏医学院	胡增青	广东茂名健康职业学院
严 璟	曲靖医学高等专科学校	夏 岚	湖北三峡职业技术学院
苏碧凤	福建卫生职业技术学院	倪 莹	潍坊护理职业学院
李 敏	雅安职业技术学院	徐 玲	四川卫生康复职业学院
李晓艳	云南新兴职业学院	徐 婧	皖西卫生职业学院
杨桂荣	湖北职业技术学院	徐毓华	江苏卫生健康职业学院
吴 梅	湖北中医药高等专科学校	唐 艳	长沙卫生职业学院
吴 敏	鄂州职业大学	黄 涛	黄河科技学院
宋华松	廊坊卫生职业学院	曹海宁	湖南环境生物职业技术学院
张 薇	重庆三峡医药高等专科学校	眭师宜	湖南中医药高等专科学校
陈 菲	江苏护理职业学院	崔 娟	青海卫生职业技术学院
陈 萍	岳阳职业技术学院	谢 涛	辽东学院
陈 敏	长春医学高等专科学校	蔺 坤	德宏职业学院
武 燕	安徽中医药高等专科学校	廖 燕	江西中医药高等专科学校
罗 琼	荆州职业技术学院	熊 锡	湘潭医卫职业技术学院

网络增值服务

使用说明

欢迎使用华中科技大学出版社医学分社资源网

1 教师使用流程

（1）登录网址：https://bookcenter.hustp.com/index.html （注册时请选择教师用户）

注册 → 登录 → 完善个人信息 → 等待审核

（2）审核通过后，您可以在网站使用以下功能：

浏览教学资源　建立课程　管理学生　布置作业　查询学生学习记录等

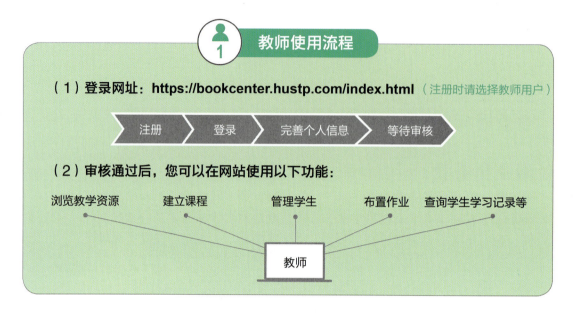

2 学员使用流程

（建议学员在PC端完成注册、登录、完善个人信息的操作）

（1）PC 端学员操作步骤

① 登录网址：https://bookcenter.hustp.com/index.html （注册时请选择普通用户）

注册 → 完善个人信息 → 登录

② 查看课程资源：（如有学习码，请在个人中心-学习码验证中先验证，再进行操作）

首页课程 →（选择课程）课程详情页 → 查看课程资源

（2）手机端扫码操作步骤

手机扫码 → 登录 → 查看数字资源 / 注册

随着我国综合国力的增强,人民生活水平不断提高,对美的需求日益提升,美容市场日益繁荣。在美容行业与国际接轨日趋紧密的情况下,美容应用英语助推美容服务国际化的作用逐渐凸显,掌握美容应用英语已经成为美容从业人员的基本工作任务之一。

《美容应用英语》依据《高等职业教育专科英语课程标准(2021年版)》专科阶段的英语拓展模块学科核心素养要求,《关于在院校实施"学历证书+若干职业技能等级证书"制度试点方案》中为学生开展X证书培训的需求,按照《"十四五"职业教育规划教材建设实施方案》,结合《高等学校课程思政建设指导纲要》编写而成,是一本美容相关专业的英语教材,适合高等职业学校医学美容技术、美容美体艺术、人物形象设计等专业使用,也适用于中高级美容师的职业培训,还可作为美容从业人员的职场参考书。

本教材共设八个单元,每个单元分为 Listening 听、Speaking 说、Reading 读、Practical Writing 实用写作四个部分,每个部分以任务导向形式展开。本教材内容以美容职业和美容项目为导向,具体涉及美容专业概况、美容前台、面部护理、身体护理、彩妆产品和化妆师、美甲,同时强调美容行业的规范意识和职业沟通能力,具体包括美容行业法律法规、沟通与服务。

本教材具有以下特色。

1. 以职场需求为导向,侧重实践与应用 本教材对接美容行业发展趋势和美容市场需求,以职业需求为导向、以实践能力培养为重点。本教材以美容前台、美容顾问、美容师、美体师、化妆师、美甲师等美容职业需求为导向,以美容院实际工作流程为线索,培养美容从业人员与客户及同事用英语进行日常会话和专业交流的能力,美容职场应用文的阅读能力和美容职场常用文体的写作能力。本教材配备大量图片,多为美容工作场景真实图片,增强了趣味性和情景性,强调教材内容与专业实践、职场需求的对接。

2. 以任务为驱动,板块完备,目标明确 每个单元内容全面,涵盖听、说、读、实用写作四大板块,满足学生深入学习美容英语的要求。每个单元设置4个或5个学习与工作任务,以任务驱动学习。每个任务前设置情景导入或背景描述;学习目标用问题形式明确提出;对话中重点语句用下划线标出;能力检测包括词语连线、选择、判断、排序、翻译、图文搭配、写作等形式，以巩固知识、提升技能，且便于教师导入题库，进行无纸化测试。各单元学习目标明确，重点突出。

3. 重视课程思政，重视职场多元文化交流 根据美容英语学科特点，每个单元融入课程思政元素，使美容英语课程与思政理论课程同向同行，努力实现美容职业技能和美容职业精神培养高度融合。加深学生对职业理念、职业责任和职业使命的认识与理解，将价值塑造、知识传授和能力培养三者融为一体，重视中国特色社会主义和中国梦宣传教育、社会主义核心价值观教育、法治教育、劳动教育、心理健康教育、中华优秀传统文化教育。帮助学生拓宽国际视野，增强文化自信，提升爱国主义情怀和民族自豪感。使学生在美容职场中能够有效进行跨文化交流，在多元文化交流中传播中华文化。

4. 数字资源完备，便于自主学习 本教材适应"互联网＋职业教育"发展需求，运用现代信息技术手段，注重培养学生自主学习和应用美容英语的能力，为终身学习和职场应用打下良好基础。本教材配备了教学PPT、音频、视频等数字资源，教师、学生等教材使用者可以通过扫描书中二维码获取相应资源，便于利用线上线下多渠道有效获取学习资源，方便自主学习。

本教材经华中科技大学出版社编辑老师大力协助，各编者所在院校鼎力支持，各兄弟美容院、美甲店倾情配合，在此一并致以诚挚感谢！本教材在编写过程中难免有疏漏之处，恳请广大读者批评指正，我们将在再版时再次完善。

编　者

目录
Contents

Unit 1　Introduction to Cosmetology
第一单元　美容专业概况　　　　　　　　　　　　　　　　/ 1

Part Ⅰ　Listening　听　　　　　　　　　　　　　　　　/ 1

　Task 1　Cosmetic Professionals
　　　　　美容职业分类　　　　　　　　　　　　　　　/ 2

Part Ⅱ　Speaking　说　　　　　　　　　　　　　　　　/ 3

　Task 2　Cosmetic Majors and Future Jobs
　　　　　美容专业和工作岗位　　　　　　　　　　　　/ 3

　Task 3　Visiting Angel Beauty Salon
　　　　　参观天使美容院　　　　　　　　　　　　　　/ 6

Part Ⅲ　Reading　读　　　　　　　　　　　　　　　　/ 8

　Task 4　Development Status of Beauty Industry
　　　　　美容行业发展现状　　　　　　　　　　　　　/ 9

Part Ⅳ　Practical Writing　实用写作　　　　　　　　　/ 10

　Task 5　Poster
　　　　　海报　　　　　　　　　　　　　　　　　　　/ 11

Unit 2　Beauty Receptionist
第二单元　美容前台　　　　　　　　　　　　　　　　　/ 16

Part Ⅰ　Listening　听　　　　　　　　　　　　　　　　/ 16

　Task 1　Communication with a New Client
　　　　　与新顾客交流　　　　　　　　　　　　　　　/ 17

Part Ⅱ　Speaking　说　　　　　　　　　　　　　　　　/ 18

　Task 2　The First Appointment of a New Client
　　　　　新顾客首次预约　　　　　　　　　　　　　　/ 19

Task 3	Phone Appointment and Post-Service Interview	
	电话预约和回访	/ 20
Part Ⅲ	Reading　读	/ 22
Task 4	Skin Health Myths to Stop Believing	
	皮肤健康的认知误区	/ 23
Part Ⅳ	Practical Writing　实用写作	/ 25
Task 5	Customer File	
	顾客档案	/ 25

Unit 3　Facial Care
第三单元　面部护理　/ 32

Part Ⅰ	Listening　听	/ 32
Task 1	Skin Care Products	
	护肤品	/ 33
Part Ⅱ	Speaking　说	/ 35
Task 2	Solutions to Skin Problems	
	皮肤问题的解决办法	/ 35
Task 3	Process of Facial Care	
	面部护理步骤	/ 37
Part Ⅲ	Reading　读	/ 40
Task 4	Operation Introduction of Photon Skin Rejuvenation Device	
	光子嫩肤仪使用说明	/ 40
Part Ⅳ	Practical Writing　实用写作	/ 43
Task 5	Ordering Letter	
	订购函	/ 44

Unit 4　Body Care
第四单元　身体护理　/ 49

Part Ⅰ	Listening　听	/ 49
Task 1	Optoelectronic Beauty Technology	
	光电美容技术	/ 50
Part Ⅱ	Speaking　说	/ 51
Task 2	Head and Neck Care	
	头颈部护理	/ 52

Task 3	Back Care	
	背部护理	/ 54
Part Ⅲ	Reading 读	/ 57
Task 4	Yin-Yang and Five Elements	
	阴阳和五行	/ 57
Part Ⅳ	Practical Writing 实用写作	/ 59
Task 5	Activity Invitation Letter	
	活动邀请函	/ 60

Unit 5　Color Cosmetics and Cosmetician
第五单元　彩妆产品和化妆师　　　　　　　　　　　/ 66

Part Ⅰ	Listening 听	/ 66
Task 1	Cosmetics Brand	
	彩妆品牌	/ 67
Part Ⅱ	Speaking 说	/ 68
Task 2	Process of Daily Makeup	
	日常妆步骤	/ 69
Task 3	Tips of Bridal Makeup	
	新娘化妆小贴士	/ 72
Part Ⅲ	Reading 读	/ 74
Task 4	Color Cosmetics Market in China	
	中国彩妆市场	/ 75
Part Ⅳ	Practical Writing 实用写作	/ 77
Task 5	Resume	
	简历	/ 77

Unit 6　Manicure
第六单元　美甲　　　　　　　　　　　　　　　　　/ 83

Part Ⅰ	Listening 听	/ 83
Task 1	The Job of a Manicurist	
	美甲师的工作	/ 84
Part Ⅱ	Speaking 说	/ 85
Task 2	Getting a Manicure	
	预约美甲	/ 86
Task 3	Process of Manicure	
	美甲	/ 88

Part Ⅲ　　Reading　读　　　　　　　　　　　　　　　　　　　/ 90
　　Task 4　Promising Future of Manicure Industry
　　　　　　美甲行业前景　　　　　　　　　　　　　　　　　/ 91
Part Ⅳ　　Practical Writing　实用写作　　　　　　　　　　　/ 93
　　Task 5　Work Schedule
　　　　　　工作计划表　　　　　　　　　　　　　　　　　　/ 94

Unit 7　Cosmetology Laws and Regulations
第七单元　美容行业法律法规　　　　　　　　　　　　　　　　 / 100

Part Ⅰ　　Listening　听　　　　　　　　　　　　　　　　　　/ 100
　　Task 1　*Safety and Technical Standards for Cosmetics*
　　　　　　《化妆品安全技术规范》　　　　　　　　　　　　　/ 101
Part Ⅱ　　Speaking　说　　　　　　　　　　　　　　　　　　/ 103
　　Task 2　Understanding the *Regulations on Supervision and Administration of Cosmetics*
　　　　　　了解《化妆品监督管理条例》　　　　　　　　　　　/ 104
Part Ⅲ　　Reading　读　　　　　　　　　　　　　　　　　　/ 107
　　Task 3　*Measures for the Administration of Medical Cosmetology Services*
　　　　　　《医疗美容服务管理办法》　　　　　　　　　　　　/ 108
Part Ⅳ　　Practical Writing　实用写作　　　　　　　　　　　/ 111
　　Task 4　Request for Leave
　　　　　　请假条　　　　　　　　　　　　　　　　　　　　/ 111

Unit 8　Communication and Service
第八单元　沟通与服务　　　　　　　　　　　　　　　　　　　/ 118

Part Ⅰ　　Listening　听　　　　　　　　　　　　　　　　　　/ 118
　　Task 1　A Process for a Massage Service
　　　　　　按摩服务流程　　　　　　　　　　　　　　　　　/ 119
Part Ⅱ　　Speaking　说　　　　　　　　　　　　　　　　　　/ 122
　　Task 2　Introducing Products
　　　　　　推介产品　　　　　　　　　　　　　　　　　　　/ 122
Part Ⅲ　　Reading　读　　　　　　　　　　　　　　　　　　/ 125
　　Task 3　Verbal Communication Skills
　　　　　　语言沟通技巧　　　　　　　　　　　　　　　　　/ 125

Task 4　Non-Verbal Communication Skills
　　　　非语言沟通技巧　　　　　　　　　　　　　　　　　　／ 128

Part Ⅳ　Practical Writing　实用写作　　　　　　　　　　　　／ 131
　Task 5　Letter of Thanks
　　　　感谢信　　　　　　　　　　　　　　　　　　　　　　／ 132

Appendix A　Vocabulary for Self-Test
附录 A　自助记忆词汇表　　　　　　　　　　　　　　　　　　／ 138

Appendix B　Common Cosmetic Brands
附录 B　常见美容产品品牌名称　　　　　　　　　　　　　　　／ 147

References
参考文献　　　　　　　　　　　　　　　　　　　　　　　　　／ 153

美容英语
词汇特点

Cosmetology Application English

Unit 1 Introduction to Cosmetology
- Task 1 Cosmetic Professionals
- Task 2 Cosmetic Majors and Future Jobs
- Task 3 Visiting Angel Beauty Salon
- Task 4 Development Status of Beauty Industry
- Task 5 Poster

Unit 2 Beauty Receptionist
- Task 1 Communication with a New Client
- Task 2 The First Appointment of a New Client
- Task 3 Phone Appointment and Post-Service Interview
- Task 4 Skin Health Myths to Stop Believing
- Task 5 Customer File

Unit 3 Facial Care
- Task 1 Skin Care Products
- Task 2 Solutions to Skin Problems
- Task 3 Process of Facial Care
- Task 4 Operation Introduction of Photon Skin Rejuvenation Device
- Task 5 Ordering Letter

Unit 4 Body Care
- Task 1 Optoelectronic Beauty Technology
- Task 2 Head and Neck Care
- Task 3 Back Care
- Task 4 Yin-Yang and Five Elements
- Task 5 Activity Invitation Letter

Unit 5 Color Cosmetics and Cosmetician
- Task 1 Cosmetics Brand
- Task 2 Process of Daily Makeup
- Task 3 Tips of Bridal Makeup
- Task 4 Color Cosmetics Market in China
- Task 5 Resume

Unit 6 Manicure
- Task 1 The Job of a Manicurist
- Task 2 Getting a Manicure
- Task 3 Process of Manicure
- Task 4 Promising Future of Manicure Industry
- Task 5 Work Schedule

Unit 7 Cosmetology Laws and Regulations
- Task 1 *Safety and Technical Standards for Cosmetics*
- Task 2 Understanding the *Regulations on Supervision and Administration of Cosmetics*
- Task 3 *Measures for the Administration of Medical Cosmetology Services*
- Task 4 Request for Leave

Unit 8 Communication and Service
- Task 1 A Process for a Massage Service
- Task 2 Introducing Products
- Task 3 Verbal Communication Skills
- Task 4 Non-Verbal Communication Skills
- Task 5 Letter of Thanks

Unit 1　Introduction to Cosmetology
第一单元　美容专业概况

扫码看
PPT

图 1-1

 Learning Objectives ▎学习目标

1. Master the expressions of cosmetic majors and future jobs.
2. Master important words and expressions in visiting Angel Beauty Salon.
3. Understand the knowledge of the development status of beauty industry.
4. Know how to write a poster.

Part Ⅰ　Listening ‖ 听

【Instruction】

Listening is a basic skill for cosmetology application English. In this part, you

will hear a short passage. It will be read twice. For extensive listening, you should be able to understand the outline of the passage. For intensive listening, the key words are important.

【Objectives】

1. First listening: Try to get the main idea of the passage.
2. Second listening: Try to grab the key words.

Task 1　Cosmetic Professionals
美容职业分类

【Description】

With the improvement of people's beauty awareness, more and more people are engaged in the beauty industry. Try to understand each bold font and choose a correct word from the **Word Bank** for each blank.

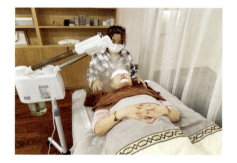

图 1-2

图 1-3

Word Bank

A. products　　B. provide　　C. regular　　D. answering　　E. body

Beautician

The main job of a beautician is to 1. _____ customers with beauty services, including face washing, massage, body care, SPA, and weight loss.

扫码听
音频 1

Beauty Adviser

The main tasks of a beauty adviser include mastering professional beauty technologies, familiarizing with the beauty service process, collecting information about the market and clients, providing clients with reasonable and proper advice, maintaining 2._____ clients and developing new clients, promoting 3._____, and handling follow-up issues of the service.

Beauty Receptionist

The main responsibilities of a beauty receptionist include 4._____ the service hotline, registering appointment information, serving customers, arranging beauticians and rooms for customers, etc.

Therapist

Therapists are mainly responsible for treating various diseases and improving conditions of the human 5._____ through various physical means.

扫码看答案 1

扫码看翻译 1

Part Ⅱ　Speaking ‖ 说

【Instruction】

Speaking is a core skill in communicating with clients, introducing programs, recommending products, etc. In this part, you will study two conversations about cosmetic majors and beauty salon.

【Objectives】

1. Master the underlined sentences for cosmetic majors and future jobs.
2. Master the underlined sentences for visiting Angel Beauty Salon.

Task 2　Cosmetic Majors and Future Jobs
美容专业和工作岗位

【Description】

Three freshmen meet at the campus. They are talking about cosmetic majors and their future jobs.

Think and discuss：

1. What is Joanna's major?

2. What does Anna want to be?

图 1-4

Mary：Hi，Anna. It's nearly half past seven. Let's go，hurry up.

Anna：All right. Today is the first day when we become college students. I'm very glad we'll meet some new classmates and teachers.

扫码听音频 2

Mary：Yes，we were in the same high school and now we are so lucky to be arranged in the same dormitory in the college. I wonder if we could meet some other old friends.

Anna：I would like to make some new friends.

Joanna：Hello，are you Mary? Do you remember me? We were schoolmates in Sunny High School.

扫码看翻译 2

Mary：Oh，yes，you are Joanna. Long time no see. Anna，this is my old friend，Joanna.

Joanna：Nice to meet you，Anna. I'm Joanna.

Anna：Nice to meet you too. What's your major?

Joanna：I'm a freshman majoring in medical cosmetic technology. What about you?

Mary：Oh，we three are in the same department. （Cheers!）I major in beauty education and management. Anna majors in traditional Chinese medicine healthcare.

Anna：Traditional Chinese medicine healthcare is my major. I want to be a skilled body therapist.

Joanna: I dream to be a beautician in a large SPA chamber. Mary, what would you like to be in the future?

Mary: I want to be a beauty adviser helping run beauty shops.

Anna: Do you intend to have your own beauty salon?

Mary: Oh, maybe. I'll consider it if I get rich experience in management and earn enough money for a beauty salon.

Joanna: Wish you make it one day!

Mary: Thank you. Oh, it's about time to have classes. Let's go.

图 1-5

Key Words and Expressions

major['meɪdʒə(r)]　n. 专业　v. 主修　adj. 主要的

freshman['freʃmən]　n. (中学或大学的)一年级新生

cosmetology[ˌkɒzməˈtɒlədʒɪ]　n. 整容术, 美容术, 美容学

cosmetic[kɒzˈmetɪk]　n. 化妆品　adj. 美容的

technology[tekˈnɒlədʒɪ]　n. 技术, 科技

department[dɪˈpɑːtmənt]　n. 系, 部门, 科室

client[ˈklaɪənt]　n. 顾客, 客户

major in　以……为专业

medical cosmetic technology　医学美容技术

beauty education and management　美容教育与管理

traditional Chinese medicine healthcare　传统中医养生

make it　及时到达, (非正式)成功

Task 3　Visiting Angel Beauty Salon
参观天使美容院

【Description】

A teacher takes several students to visit Angel Beauty Salon. The beauty receptionist Betty and the beauty adviser Mary are receiving them.

Think and discuss:

1. What is the disinfection cabinet used for?
2. How many beds are there in the salon?

图 1-6

Betty: Hello, welcome to Angel Beauty Salon. I'm Betty, the beauty receptionist.

Teacher: Hello, Betty, would you like to show us around your beauty salon?

扫码听音频 3

Betty: It would be my pleasure. Now, we're in the reception room. Our clients can take a rest and discuss their needs with our beauty adviser as well.

Student 1: Oh, it's decorated just like a four-star hotel. The clients may feel very relaxed in such a delightful ambiance.

Betty: Yes, you said it.

扫码看翻译 3

Student 2: I'm willing to work in such a comfortable environment from the bottom of my heart.

Teacher: Very well. This is one of the reasons why I show you this beauty salon.

Betty: Excuse me, I have to answer a phone call. Mary will continue to show you around our beauty salon.

Mary: Hello, I'm Mary, a beauty adviser. This way, please. This is the batching room for preparing materials.

Student 3: Great! Wow, you have a disinfection cabinet here.

Mary: Yes, our disinfection cabinet is generally used to disinfect used items such as towels, bath towels and sheets.

Student 3: That certainly makes the customer feel at ease.

Mary: Absolutely!

Student 1: Wow, you see, the crystal lamp on the ceiling is so beautiful! And the mirror in front of the dressing table is really big!

Mary: Thank you for your compliment. All of the interior decorations are carefully chosen by our salon manager. We not only want to help bring out the beauty and good health in every client, but also would like to make the client feel well pampered. Clients will dress themselves up here. If necessary, we also provide makeup and manicure. Of course, there are additional service fees for that. This way, please.

Student 2: Are these all beauty treatment rooms? How many beds are there in your salon?

Mary: Um, 25 beds. There are five three-bed and four double-bed rooms. We also have two single-bed rooms that are specially designed for our VIP clients.

Student 1: What service programs do you offer?

Mary: The most common programs are facial care and body care. Besides, we also offer other services such as aromatherapy, SPA beauty treatment and hydrotherapy, and various makeup and manicure. All of our beauticians have got vocational beautician certificates.

Student 3: It's not easy to be a qualified beautician. We have to study hard to pass the national beautician vocational skill examination.

Mary: May your dreams come true.

Students: Thank you very much!

Mary: Not at all!

Key Words and Expressions

angel['eɪndʒl]   n. 天使,天使般的人
salon['sælɒn]   n. 客厅,沙龙

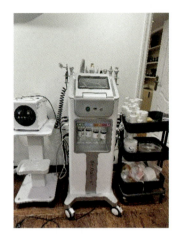
图 1-7

图 1-8

decorate['dekəreɪt]　v. 装饰, 布置, 装修
relaxation[ˌriːlæk'seɪʃn]　n. 放松, 消遣, 松弛
elegant['elɪɡənt]　adj. 优雅的, 雅致的
comfortable['kʌmftəbl]　adj. 令人舒适的, 安逸的
environment[ɪn'vaɪrənmənt]　n. 环境, 外界, 周围
charge[tʃɑːdʒ]　v. 要价　n. 责任, 费用
double['dʌbl]　adj. 双重的, 成双的
beauty salon/shop　美容院
reception room　接待室, 接待区
dressing table　梳妆台
batching room　配料间
show sb. around　带(某人)参观

Part Ⅲ　Reading ‖ 读

【Instruction】

For a beauty practitioner, reading especially extensive reading is a necessary skill. In this part, you will study a text related to the development status of beauty industry.

【Objectives】

1. Find the topic sentence for each paragraph.

2. Try to get the main idea of the text.

Task 4　Development Status of Beauty Industry
美容行业发展现状

【Description】

Nowadays, with the continuous improvement of people's awareness of beauty and health care, the number of beauty salons is increasing. Therefore, the cosmetic major as an employment direction is a good choice with good prospects.

图 1-9

In recent years, with the increasing demand for beauty, the beauty industry has developed rapidly. At present, the beauty industry mainly includes cosmetics, beauty and hairdressing, medical cosmetology and other sub-industries. Let's take a look at the current development status of the beauty industry.

扫码听音频 4

First of all, the cosmetics industry is the most important sub-industry in the beauty industry. With the constant improvement of people's requirements for product quality, the cosmetics industry is constantly innovating, adding more functional products made of natural ingredients, so that consumers can feel assured to use them.

扫码看翻译 4

Secondly, the beauty and hairdressing industry is also developing rapidly. With more attention on their images and health, consumers begin to pay more attention to personalized beauty and hairdressing services. At present, its market size in China has exceeded 500 billion yuan and is still expanding.

Finally, medical cosmetology industry is one of the most rapidly developing sub-industries in recent years. With the growth of people's age and the requirements of external image, more and more people begin to choose medical cosmetology services.

In short, the development prospects of the beauty industry in China are very broad, and there is still great space for development.

图 1-10

Key Words and Expressions

status['steɪtəs]　n.(进展的)状况,地位,身份
constant['kɒnstənt]　adj.不断的,连续发生的
innovate['ɪnəveɪt]　v.革新,创新
functional['fʌŋkʃənl]　adj.实用的,功能的
ingredient[ɪn'griːdiənt]　n.(食品的)成分,原料
pay attention to　对(某人/某事)注意
in short　总之,简言之

Part Ⅳ　Practical Writing ‖ 实用写作

【Instruction】

In working scenario, a beauty practitioner will come across practical writing on some particular occasions. In this part, you will study a main form of beauty practical writing—poster.

【Objective】

Know how to write a poster.

Task 5　Poster
海报

【Description】

Posters can be used for beauty salon openings, anniversary celebrations, project promotion activities, etc.

Structure:

A poster usually consists of three parts:

1. the subject

2. the body (details like activity, time, place, etc.)

3. the signature (organizer)

Model:

Academic Lecture Poster

Topic: Home Skin Care Guide

Speaker: Prof. Zhao

Time: From 14:30 to 16:30 on Thursday, April 14

Place: Meeting room on the third floor

All beauticians are expected to attend the lecture.

Angel Beauty Salon

April 10, 2022

Summarize 项目小结

In this unit we have learnt:

1. Some majors of cosmetology.

2. Knowledge about a beauty salon.

3. Knowledge about the development status of beauty industry.

4. How to write a poster.

Test Yourself 能力检测

1. Match each English word or expression in Column A with its Chinese meaning in Column B based on Task 1.

Column A	Column B
(1) register	A. 客户
(2) beautician	B. 服务
(3) client	C. 预约
(4) service	D. 登记
(5) appointment	E. 减肥
(6) collect	F. 信息
(7) information	G. 身体的
(8) therapist	H. 理疗师
(9) physical	I. 收集
(10) weight loss	J. 美容师

扫码看
答案 2

2. Look at these pictures and point out what the jobs are based on Task 1.

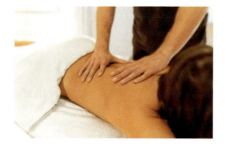

图 1-11 _____

图 1-12 _____

图 1-13 _____

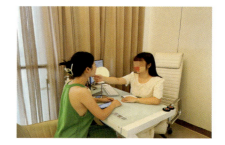

图 1-14 _____

3. Decide whether the statement is true(T) or false(F) based on Task 2.

____(1) Mary and Joanna are old friends since high school.

____(2) These three girls were classmates in middle school.

____(3) They are in the same major.

____(4) Joanna's major is traditional Chinese medicine healthcare.

____(5) Anna wants to be a body therapist.

4. Decide whether the statement is true(T) or false(F) based on Task 3.

____(1) Today we'll visit Angel Beauty Salon so that we can work there.

____(2) Betty is a beauty adviser.

____(3) Clients can have a talk with the beauty adviser in the reception room.

____(4) Services such as makeup and manicure are free in Angel Beauty Salon.

____(5) It is very easy to be a qualified beautician.

5. Choose the proper translation for each phrase based on Task 4.

(1) _____ beauty salon

(2) _____ natural ingredient

(3) _____ 5000 亿元

(4) _____ 医美

(5) _____ 个性化服务

A. personalized service

B. 500 billion yuan

C. medical cosmetology

D. 天然成分

E. 美容院

6. Writing practice based on Task 5.

说明：××美容院将于 7 月 6 日上午 10:00 在福达广场一楼举办 5 周年庆典，届时将有回馈活动和礼品，欢迎新老顾客参加。请用英语写一则活动海报。

课程思政　Curriculum Ideology and Politics

传统文化赏析：*The Reed*《蒹葭》

蒹葭	The Reed
蒹葭苍苍，白露为霜。	Green, green the reed, dew and frost gleam.
所谓伊人，在水一方。	Where's she I need? Beyond the stream.
溯洄从之，道阻且长。	Upstream I go, the way is long.
溯游从之，宛在水中央。	Downstream I go, she's there among.
蒹葭萋萋，白露未晞。	White, white the reed, dew not yet dried.
所谓伊人，在水之湄。	Where's she I need? On the other side.
溯洄从之，道阻且跻。	Upstream I go, hard is the way.
溯游从之，宛在水中坻。	Downstream I go, she's far away.
蒹葭采采，白露未已。	Bright, bright the reed, dew and frost blend.
所谓伊人，在水之涘。	Where's she I need? At river's end.
溯洄从之，道阻且右。	Upstream I go, the way does wind.
溯游从之，宛在水中沚。	Downstream I go, she's far behind.

图 1-15

Key Words and Expressions

dew[dju:]　n. 露水

frost[frɒst]　n. 霜，严寒天气

gleam[gli:m] v. 发微光,闪烁
upstream[ˌʌp'stri:m] adv. 向(在)上游,逆流地
downstream[ˌdaʊn'stri:m] adv. 向(在)下游,顺流地
not yet 也不,还没有

扫码看视频

（徐　曼　余芊芊）

Unit 2　Beauty Receptionist
第二单元　美容前台

图 2-1

Learning Objectives　学习目标

1. Master the expressions of beauty receptionist etiquette.
2. Master the expressions of beauty receptionist conversation.
3. Know how to communicate with clients.
4. Know how to write a customer file.

Part Ⅰ　Listening　听

【Instruction】

Listening is a basic skill for cosmetology application English. In this part, you

will hear a short dialogue. It will be read twice. For extensive listening, you should be able to understand the outline of the dialogue. For intensive listening, the key words are important.

【Objectives】

1. First listening: Try to get the main idea of the dialogue.

2. Second listening: Try to answer the following questions.

(1) What is the client's name? Please spell it.

(2) When is the appointment?

3. Try to grab the key words.

Task 1　Communication with a New Client
　　　　与新顾客交流

【Description】

A beauty receptionist is communicating with a new client by phone. Choose a correct word from the **Word Bank** for each blank.

图 2-2

> **Word Bank**
> A. appointment　　B. fill out　　C. assisting　　D. spell　　E. reservation

A: Hi! Is it Angel Beauty Salon?

B: Hi! Yes, I'm Betty from Angel Beauty Salon. What can I do for you?

A: I would like to check my 1. _____.

B: You have a(an) 2. _____ with us, right?

A: Yes, I do.

B: OK. What is it?

A: Um?

B: I mean your name.

A: Oh, right. This is Hannah.

B: Could you 3. _____ it out for me?

A: H-A-N-N-A-H.

B: Got it. Thank you. So it seems that you have an appointment with Dr. Johnson at 15:00 today, but he is currently 4. _____ another client, so you may have to wait for a little bit. Would you please come at 15:30?

A: OK.

B: While you wait, please 5. _____ the client's information form for me. I'll send it to you through WeChat.

A: Sure. Where should I fill in?

B: It's right at the bottom. Thank you.

扫码看答案 1

扫码看翻译 1

Part Ⅱ Speaking ‖ 说

【Instruction】

Speaking is a core skill in communicating with clients, introducing programs, recommending products, etc. In this part, you will study two conversations about the first appointment of a new client and the post-service interview.

【Objective】

Master the underlined sentences for appointment and post-service interview.

Task 2　The First Appointment of a New Client
新顾客首次预约

【Description】

A client comes to inquire about some promotional campaigns of Angel Beauty Salon. The beauty receptionist is introducing beauty programs and promotions.

Think and discuss:

1. What skills should a beautician have?
2. How to introduce a promotional campaign or a beauty program?

图 2-3

Betty—a beauty receptionist　　Eliza—a new client

Betty: Hello, this is Angel Beauty Salon. I'm Betty. Can I help you?

Eliza: Hello, I'm Eliza. Yesterday I received a leaflet of your beauty salon in front of the supermarket. It is said that you are having some promotional campaigns because of annual celebration. Is it true?

Betty: Yes, this month we'll have our eighth annual celebration. We are having promotional campaigns to pay back our regular clients' great support during these years, and we also set up some programs for new clients. Would you like to become our new client?

Eliza: Um... Let me think about it. What are your promotional campaigns?

扫码听
音频 2

扫码看
翻译 2

Betty: You can experience a facial treatment with 50% discount. Our beauty adviser will test and analyze your skin condition for free and give you some advice on how to choose and use skin care products to promote your skin quality. When will you be free to come here?

Eliza: Mm, maybe tomorrow afternoon. In autumn, my skin is very dry, and I want to know how to keep moisturized.

Betty: No problem. We have some good quality lotion and cream for retaining moisture. There are also some facial treatment programs for retaining moisture in autumn.

Eliza: Oh, I hope so. Bye-bye.

Betty: Wait for a minute, please. Would you tell us your telephone or mobile phone number? I'll call you in advance to remind you tomorrow morning.

Eliza: My mobile phone number is 138××××××××. I'm sure to come tomorrow. See you.

Betty: See you tomorrow.

Key Words and Expressions

receptionist[rɪˈsepʃnɪst]　n. 接待员
leaflet[ˈliːflət]　n. 宣传单
promote[prəˈməʊt]　v. 促进，推动
moisture[ˈmɔɪstʃə(r)]　n. 滋润
discount[ˈdɪskaʊnt]　n. 折扣
pay back　回馈
regular client　老顾客，常客
facial treatment　面部护理
promotional campaigns　促销活动

Task 3　Phone Appointment and Post-Service Interview
　　　　　电话预约和回访

【Description】

The following conversation is between a client (Diana Smith) and Betty who is a beauty receptionist in Angel Beauty Salon.

Think and discuss:

1. What could you do to help a client to make an appointment?
2. When should you do a post-service interview? What will you say then?

图 2-4

Betty—a beauty receptionist   Diana Smith—a client

Betty: Hello, this is Angel Beauty Salon. I'm Betty, a beauty receptionist. What can I do for you?

Diana Smith: This is Diana Smith. I want to do facial care at 2:00 this afternoon. Can I ask Alice to do it for me?

Betty: You said you'd like to come at 2:00 pm, right? Let me check the reservation list. Oh, sorry, Alice has an appointment with another client at that time. May I arrange another beautician for you today? How about Anna? She's a new beautician, but…

Diana Smith: Sorry, I don't accept a newcomer. Alice is the only one.

Betty: Anna is the champion of provincial cosmetology competition this year. She is very good at massage and acupressure. You sound a bit tired and really need a relaxation. Would you have a try this time?

Diana Smith: Yes, I would. I'm really exhausted.

Betty: OK. We'll wait for your coming at 2:00 pm. See you then.

Diana Smith: See you.

(*The next day, Betty interviews Mrs. Smith in the phone.*)

Betty: Hello, this is Betty of Angel Beauty Salon. Is that Mrs. Smith?

Diana Smith: It's me.

Betty: How did you feel about Anna's service yesterday?

Diana Smith: It's wonderful. I haven't been so relaxed recently. I had a good sleep that afternoon. Thank you very much.

扫码听
音频 3

扫码看
翻译 3

Betty: You're welcome. Do you remember to have moisturizing masks regularly at home?

Diana Smith: Yes, I do it once every three days. I feel my skin is more moisturized than before.

Betty: Excellent! Will you come at the same time next week?

Diana Smith: Yes, if I'm free.

Betty: All right, I'll send a short message to remind you on Monday.

Diana Smith: Thank you for everything you've done. Good-bye.

Betty: You are welcome. Bye-bye.

图 2-5

Key Words and Expressions

reservation [ˌrezəˈveɪʃn] n. 预订
arrange [əˈreɪndʒ] v. 安排
beautician [bjuːˈtɪʃn] n. 美容师
provincial [prəˈvɪnʃəl] adj. 省级的
acupressure [ˈækjupreʃə(r)] n. 指压

Part Ⅲ Reading ‖ 读

【Instruction】

For a beauty receptionist, reading especially extensive reading is a necessary skill. In this part, you will study the introduction about skin health myths to stop believing.

【Objectives】

1. Find the topic sentence for each paragraph.
2. Try to get the main idea of the text.
3. Master the underlined sentences.

Task 4 Skin Health Myths to Stop Believing
皮肤健康的认知误区

【Description】

All of us are concerned about skin health, especially ladies. It's important to get some skin care tips in our daily life. The tips in the following introduction maybe help some of you.

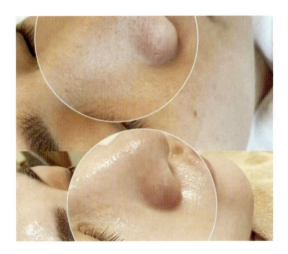

图 2-6

Betty—a beauty adviser   Diana Smith—a client

Diana Smith: Could you tell me some tips about skin care?

Betty: Yes, I just tell you some skin health myths to stop believing. Maybe it will be helpful. We all put a lot of importance into caring for our skin, which makes sense, since it's the first thing other people see. Skin might also be one of the most misunderstood parts of our bodies, so today I'd like to run through some of the most common myths we have about our skin.

Myth number one—healthy skin is skin that looks flawless. When we think of

图 2-7

healthy skin, we might think of a clear, even surface that's radiant and devoid of blemishes. But skin is a living organ, just like other organs. It's complex and serves many functions, but not just about what's going on at the surface.

Myth number two—we only need sunscreen on sunny days. Our skin has a defense system. When it's exposed to UV, we get a tan.

Myth number three—people with darker skin don't need sunscreen. It's true that having more melanin can offer some stronger protection from the sun. We do have some SPF, but it's not nearly enough. We all need sunscreen to ward off damage.

Myth number four—we can shrink our pores. Pores are the tiny openings in our skin. Pore size is largely determined by genetics.

Myth number five—chocolate causes acne. There are a lot of factors involved in complex circumstances, but research suggests that the healthiest diet for your body overall could also be the healthiest diet for your skin.

扫码听音频

扫码看翻译

Key Words and Expressions

radiant [ˈreɪdiənt]　adj. 容光焕发的
blemish [ˈblemɪʃ]　n. 斑点，瑕疵　v. 破坏……的完美
organ [ˈɔːgən]　n. 器官
function [ˈfʌŋkʃn]　n. 功能
sunscreen [ˈsʌnskriːn]　n. 防晒霜（油）
melanin [ˈmelənɪn]　n. 黑色素
tan [tæn]　n. 棕褐色肤色　v. 晒黑

ward[wɔːd]　v. 躲开，避开，防止
shrink[ʃrɪŋk]　v. 收缩
genetics[dʒə'netɪks]　n. 遗传学，遗传特征
acne['æknɪ]　n. 痤疮，粉刺
diet['daɪət]　n. 日常饮食
make sense　合乎情理
ward off　躲开，避开，防止

Part Ⅳ　Practical Writing ‖ 实用写作

【Instruction】

In working scenario, a beauty practitioner will come across practical writing on some particular occasions. In this part, you will study a main form of beauty practical writing—customer file.

【Objective】

Know how to write a customer file.

Task 5　Customer File
顾客档案

【Description】

Customer file is very important for a beauty adviser to get the customer's skin information.

Structure：

A customer file usually consists of three parts：

1. the title(such as Customer File)

2. the description of customer's skin(details like dry skin/oily skin, etc.)

3. kinds of beauty items

Example：

The following chart is a standard example of basic information in a customer file. The words and phrases in the **Word Bank** are for reference.

图 2-8

> **Word Bank**
> 1. oily(dry) skin 油(干)性皮肤
> 2. normal skin 正常皮肤
> 3. mixed skin 混合型皮肤
> 4. facelift 面部提拉
> 5. acne blemish treatment 痤疮治疗
> 6. redness relief 舒缓泛红
> 7. face purifying 面部清洁
> 8. exfoliating 去角质

Customer File

Name					
Age		Weight		Occupation	
Telephone					
Address					

Skin Type:

Health Status:

Types of Skin Care Treatment:

Summarize 项目小结

In this unit we have learnt:

1. How to make an appointment and a post-service interview with a client.
2. Knowledge about how to introduce some tips about skin care.
3. How to write a customer file.

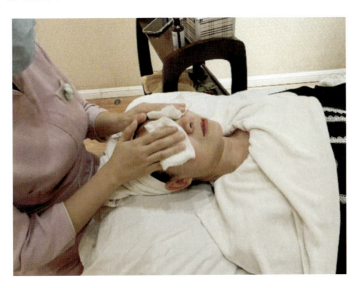

图 2-9

Test Yourself 能力检测

1. Match each English word or expression in Column A with its Chinese meaning in Column B based on Task 1.

Column A	Column B
(1) normal skin	A. 油(干)性皮肤
(2) oil(dry) skin	B. 接待员
(3) receptionist	C. 顾客
(4) client	D. 面部护理
(5) facial treatment	E. 正常皮肤
(6) appointment	F. 表格
(7) form	G. 沙龙
(8) salon	H. 预约

扫码看
答案 2

2. Look at these pictures and match each picture with a proper item based on Task 2.

(1) face mask _____

(2) foaming cleanser _____

(3) sunscreen _____

(4) lotion _____

(5) face serum _____

(6) eye cream _____

(7) face cream _____

图 2-10(选项 A)

图 2-11(选项 B)

图 2-12(选项 C)

图 2-13(选项 D)

图 2-14(选项 E)

图 2-15(选项 F)

图 2-16(选项 G)

3. Fill in the form based on Task 3.

Client's Name	Appointed Time	Program	Beautician's Name	Receptionist's Name	Note

4. Read the dialogue in pairs and then fill in the missing words.

A: Hello, This is Betty of Angel Beauty Salon. Is that Mrs. Smith?

B: It's me.

A: How did you feel about Anna's service yesterday?

B: (1)_____. I haven't been so relaxed recently. I had a good sleep that afternoon. Thank you very much.

A:(2)_____. Do you remember to have moisturizing masks regularly at home?

B:Yes,I do it (3)_____. I feel my skin is more moisturized than before.

A:Excellent! Will you come to our beauty salon (4)_____ next week?

B:Yes,(5)_____.

A:All right,I'll send you a short message to remind you on Monday.

B:OK. Good-bye.

A:Bye.

5. Decide whether the statement is true(T) or false(F) based on Task 4.

____(1) Healthy skin is a clear, even surface that's radiant and devoid of blemishes.

____(2) You only need sunscreen on sunny days.

____(3) People with darker skin also need sunscreen.

____(4) Pores are the tiny openings in our skin, so we can shrink them.

____(5) Chocolate causes acne.

6. Translate the following terms or sentences based on Task 4.

(1) Skin health myths to stop believing.

_____

(2) When skin is exposed to UV, we get a tan.

_____

(3) Skin is complex and serves many functions, but not just about what's going on at the surface.

_____

(4) Pore size is largely determined by genetics.

_____

(5) The healthiest diet for your body overall could also be the healthiest diet for your skin.

_____

(6) 接待礼仪_____

(7) 面部清洁_____

(8) 痤疮治疗_____

(9) 混合型皮肤_____

(10) 舒缓泛红_____

7. Match each English word or expression in Column A with its Chinese meaning in Column B based on Task 1 to Task 5.

Column A	Column B
(1) pay back	A. 合乎情理
(2) organ	B. 避开,躲避
(3) exfoliating	C. 遗传学
(4) leaflet	D. 黑色素
(5) genetics	E. 收缩
(6) ward off	F. 美容学
(7) melanin	G. 宣传单
(8) make sense	H. 去角质
(9) blemish	I. 器官
(10) cosmetology	J. 瑕疵
(11) shrink	K. 安排
(12) arrange	L. 反馈,回报

8. Writing practice based on Task 5.

说明:假设你的顾客叫Jean,35岁,女性,教师,家住东湖区,联系电话576831。她第一次来做面部护理,干性皮肤。她需要做清洁、保湿等面部护理。请你尝试给她建立一份顾客档案。格式如下:

Customer File

Name					
Age		Weight		Occupation	
Telephone					
Address					

Skin Type:

Health Status:

Types of Skin Care Treatment:

课程思政 Curriculum Ideology and Politics

Reception Etiquette   接待礼仪

1. Reception "4S" Principle

Smile, speed, smart, and sincerity.

图 2-17

2. Principles Followed by Service Personnel

The customer is always right. When in doubt, please understand and smile.

3. Grooming Standard

Keep clean.

Make up for a natural look.

Uniform must be neat and fit well.

Name badge should be worn on top left-hand side.

The use of very strong pungent perfume is not permitted.

扫码看
翻译 5

Key Words and Expressions

principle [ˈprɪnsɪpəl]　n. 原则
uniform [ˈjuːnɪfɔːm]　n. 制服
name badge　名牌，工牌
strong pungent　强烈刺鼻的

（李　琳　余芊芊）

Unit 3　Facial Care
第三单元　面部护理

图 3-1

Learning Objectives | 学习目标

1. Master the expressions of skin care products.
2. Master the expressions of solutions to skin problems and process of facial care.
3. Understand the operation introduction of photon skin rejuvenation device.
4. Know how to write an ordering letter.

Part Ⅰ　Listening ‖ 听

【Instruction】

Listening is a basic skill for cosmetology application English. In this part, you

will hear two short dialogues. They will be read twice. For extensive listening, you should be able to understand the outline of the dialogues. For intensive listening, the key words are important.

【Objectives】

1. First listening: Try to get the main idea of the dialogues.
2. Second listening: Try to grab the key words.

Task 1　Skin Care Products
护肤品

【Description】

There are many kinds of skin care products. We should learn to identify them and choose the products suitable for our skin. Choose a correct word or phrase from the **Word Bank** for each blank.

图 3-2

Word Bank

A. paste　　　　　　　B. powder　　　　　　　C. Neuter
D. cream　　　　　　　E. lotion　　　　　　　　F. acne-prone skin
G. facial cleanser　　　H. skin care products　　I. moisturize
J. soft cleanser

Identifying Cosmetics

Eliza—a client   Mary—a beauty adviser

Eliza: There are large categories of cosmetics, how do you divide them?

Mary: Well, according to the shape, cosmetics can be divided into 1._____, oil, 2._____, 3._____ and 4._____. We can also divide them into three types by effects: cleansing products, 5._____ and decoration cosmetics.

Facial Cleanser

B—a beautician   C—a client

B: Hello!

C: Hi! I want to buy a 6._____. I do not know which one suits me.

B: OK. I will first detect your skin. I can recommend you to buy an appropriate skin care product according to your skin type. Your skin is very white and delicate, but the skin is relatively dry. Because of water shortage, the eyes have small fine lines, so your skin belongs to dry skin. You can choose the skin care product which can 7._____ and hydrate your skin.

C: Oh, which facial cleanser is suitable for me?

B: Facial cleanser is used for cleaning and protecting your skin. Facial cleanser can be divided into two types: 8._____ and oily facial cleanser. Soft cleanser contains mild formula which is suitable for neutral, dry and sensitive skin, and the formula of oily facial cleanser contains less fat. After washing your face with oily facial cleanser, your facial skin feels very clean, so it's suitable for oily and 9._____. 10._____ or dry skin can't use oily facial cleanser, because it can make skin drier and dehydrated. Therefore, dry skin should choose soft cleanser.

C: OK.

B: This cleanser is rich in foam and is the best choice for dry skin. The product contains sweet almond essence, which can clean the dirt on the face, enhance skin vigor and make the skin moist and not dry.

C: Good! That's it!

扫码看
答案1

扫码看
翻译1

Part Ⅱ　Speaking ‖ 说

【Instruction】

Speaking is a core skill in communicating with clients, talking about the skin problems, giving some proper advice, introducing process of skin care, etc. In this part, you will study two conversations about facial care.

【Objectives】

1. Master the underlined sentences for identifying skin types and giving solutions to skin problems.

2. Master the underlined sentences for the process of facial care.

Task 2　Solutions to Skin Problems
　　　　皮肤问题的解决办法

【Description】

The beauty adviser is having a talk with the clients on skin problems and assisting them to identify their skin types, and then gives them proper advice to solve the skin problems.

Think and discuss:

1. What types of skin are there?

2. Do you know your skin type? How to solve the different skin problems?

扫码听
音频 2

扫码看
翻译 2

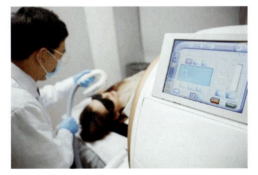

图 3-3

Mary—a beauty adviser   Ida, Eliza, Grace and Diana Smith—clients

Mary: Hello, I'm Mary, a beauty adviser here. As we know, people have different types of skin. Ida, do you know what types of skin are there?

Ida: There are five types of skin: dry, oily, normal, mixed and sensitive.

Mary: Absolutely right. We can check our skin type with this skin analysis apparatus. Actually, we can also simply know our skin type by observing how much oil our skin produces. Ida, do you know your skin type?

Ida: I have oily skin. Just as many young boys and girls, I have many pimples and acne on my forehead and nose.

图 3-4   图 3-5

Mary: You are prone to form acne skin and you'd better pay more attention to skin cleansing and choose light lotion or cream. Remember to eat less spicy food. Eliza, how about you?

Eliza: I am prone to have red spots when I try new products or eat seafood, especially shrimps.

Mary: Obviously, your skin is sensitive. You ought to be cautious to choose and use soft skin care products and eat less seafood.

Grace: I'm Grace, maybe my skin is dry. I pat much toner every day, but my skin is still dry. What should I do?

Mary: You should add oil as well as water so as to keep the balance of water and oil in your skin.

Diana Smith: I also feel my skin is dry and tight.

Mary: Mrs. Smith, you are dry on the cheeks while oily on the T-zone, so you have mixed skin.

Diana Smith: Oh, what should I do?

Mary: It's very important to replenish water and keep moisture at any time, especially for people with dry and mixed skin. It's better to have moisturizing masks daily or at least three times a week.

Diana Smith: Thank you.

Mary: My pleasure.

图 3-6

Key Words and Expressions

analysis[ə'næləsɪs]   n. 分析，解析
apparatus[ˌæpə'reɪtəs]   n. 器官，装置，机构，组织，仪器
spicy['spaɪsɪ]   adj. 辣的
shrimp[ʃrɪmp]   n. 虾
cautious['kɔːʃəs]   adj. 小心的，谨慎的，慎重的
cheek[tʃiːk]   n. 面颊
moisturize['mɔɪstʃəraɪz]   v. 给……增加水分，使……湿润
skin analysis apparatus   皮肤分析仪
be prone to   倾向于……

Task 3　Process of Facial Care
　　　　面部护理步骤

【Description】

The beauty adviser is arranging a beautician to give a facial care for the client.
Think and discuss：
1. What is the function of a cosmetic sprayer?
2. What is the process of facial care?

Mary—a beauty adviser　Diana Smith—a client　Anna—a beautician
Mary greets Mrs. Smith and arranges Anna to give a facial care for Mrs. Smith.
　　Anna：I'm Anna. This way please, Mrs. Smith. Please take off your coat,

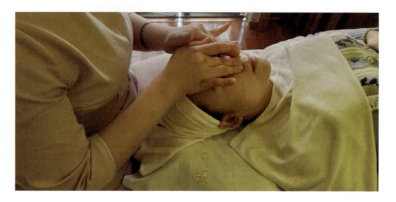

图 3-7

necklace and earrings, and put on this gown. Lie down, please. Wait for a moment. I'll prepare materials and equipment for you.

(*After a moment, Anna comes back.*)

Diana Smith: What's this?

Anna: It's a cosmetic sprayer. It will be helpful to open your facial pore to let the dirt and the waste out and nutrient into the skin.

扫码听
音频 3

Diana Smith: Oh, I see. What will you do during facial care?

Anna: First, I'll give you a makeup removal and then select a gentle cleansing lotion to clean your face. After the cleansing stage, I'll have an exfoliation with scrubbing cream for you. Do you know when you had your last exfoliation?

扫码看
翻译 3

Diana Smith: Last week.

Anna: You really haven't much oil on your face, so we needn't do it this time. But there are some comedones on your nose. Would you allow me to get rid of them? You'll feel a little pain.

Diana Smith: If you do it slightly, I can bear it.

Anna: Believe me, I'll do it carefully. After cleansing and exfoliation, I will massage your face with essential oil for 15-20 minutes and then apply a facial mask. If you have time today, I can give you an eye care.

Diana Smith: How long will they last?

Anna: Two hours together.

Diana Smith: OK. I will do both this time. I would like to have a sleep for a while, so don't talk to me anymore.

Anna: I see. Have a good rest. While cleansing and massaging, please tell me if the pressure is too heavy or too light. How are you feeling now, Madam?

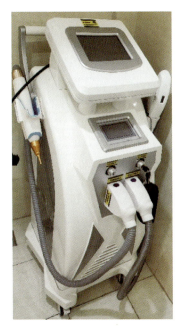 

图 3-8 图 3-9

Diana Smith: Very comfortable, thank you.

(Two hours later, Anna removed the mask for Mrs. Smith.)

Anna: Could you see anything clearly?

Diana Smith: No, I feel a bit faint.

Anna: Well. I will wipe up residue in your eyes. How are you feeling now?

Diana Smith: Much better.

Anna: Now, I have applied some toning lotion, essence, day cream and sunscreen on your face. Most of them will soon be absorbed. Would you get up or still lie down for a rest?

Diana Smith: Um, I would like to get up and please give me my coat.

Anna: Here you are.

Diana Smith: Thank you. I really have a good sleep today.

Anna: Wonderful! Please have a glass of water. You look very refreshed now.

Diana Smith: Thank you for your excellent service.

Anna: Don't mention it. Please sign your name at the reception desk. Mary is waiting for you. Remember to come here next week.

Diana Smith: I will. See you next time.

Anna: See you.

Key Words and Expressions

necklace[ˈnekləs]　n. 项链
earring[ˈɪərɪŋ]　n. 耳环
gown[ɡaʊn]　n. 长袍
sprayer[ˈspreɪə(r)]　n. 喷雾机
exfoliation[ˌeksˌfəʊlɪˈeɪʃn]　n. 去角质
massage[ˈmæsɑːʒ]　n. 按摩，推拿　v. 按摩，推拿
faint[feɪnt]　adj. 微弱的，模糊的，暗淡的
residue[ˈrezɪdjuː]　n. 残渣，剩余物
refreshed[rɪˈfreʃt]　adj. 精力充沛的，恢复活力的
scrubbing cream　磨砂膏
essential oil　精油

Part Ⅲ　Reading ‖ 读

【Instruction】

For a beauty practitioner, reading especially extensive reading is a necessary skill. In this part, you will study a text related to facial care.

【Objectives】

1. Understand the operation introduction of facial care device.
2. Try to get the main expression of the device instruction.

Task 4　Operation Introduction of Photon Skin Rejuvenation Device
光子嫩肤仪使用说明

【Description】

Photon skin rejuvenation device is a kind of device designed for facial beautification and commonly used during daily facial care.

图 3-10

Product features and functions:

1. Seven-color LED mask can solve stubborn skin problems, such as healing acne and repairing the acne scar.

2. Boost collagen and tighten skin. Reduce and prevent wrinkles. Help to fight fatty areas.

3. The intensity and the time can be adjusted by using the romote.

4. It can lessen fine lines and wrinkles around forehead and eyes in just 4-6 weeks by using for about 20 minutes each day.

5. The photon beauty device, designed for facial beautification, uses natural light waves, which are transmitted into the skin by LED. The light activates photoreceptors in skin cells, and produces energy for absorption by skin components, so as to beautify your complexion.

Seven-color LED mask can solve stubborn skin problems:

470 nm-LED blue light: Efficiently minimize and heal acne, and repair the skin without leaving scars.	
520 nm-LED green light: Neutralize and balance skin condition, relieve mental stress, and effectively dredge lymphedema.	
590 nm-LED yellow light: Improve coarseness, wrinkle, redness and fever of the skin, and increase immunity.	

续表

630 nm-LED red light： Whiten pale spot, tender skin and resist wrinkle, repair damaged skin, smooth the fine wrinkles, shrink pores, and increase collagen.	
LED purple light： It is red and blue dual-band light, having a combination of two kinds of phototherapy effect. It is especially effective in healing and repairing the acne scar.	
LED green blue light： Enhance the energy uptake by cells gradually and promote metabolism.	
LED laser light(white light)： Resolve age spots, improve fine lines and saggy skin.	

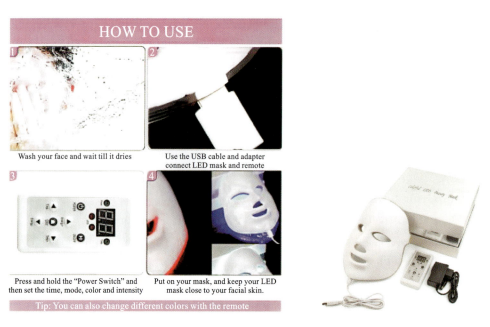

图 3-11　　　　　　　　　　　　图 3-12

How to use：

1. Plug the USB connector at the end of the wire of the LED mask.

2. Wash your face and wait till it dries. This makes it easier for light to penetrate your skin.

3. Put on the LED mask. Make sure that you wear it comfortably.

4. Turn on the LED mask and you will see tinge of red light covering the whole mask.

Note: The light is at low-level intensity. You may close your eyes if you feel a little unwell.

5. Keep the LED mask close to your facial skin.

Included:

1×LED mask

1×remote

1×power cord

1×full English user manual

Key Words and Expressions

stubborn['stʌbən]　adj. 有决心的, 顽强的, 坚持不懈的
tighten['taɪtn]　v. 拉紧, 拽紧, 加强, 强化
adjust[ə'dʒʌst]　v. 调整, 调好, 整理, 评定, 适应
beautification[ˌbjuːtɪfɪ'keɪʃn]　n. 美化
complexion[kəm'plekʃn]　n. 肤色, 面色, 性质, 气质
plug[plʌg]　v. 填塞, 插入
penetrate['penɪtreɪt]　v. 透入, 渗入, 透过
photon skin rejuvenation device　光子嫩肤仪
stubborn skin problems　顽固的皮肤问题
user manual　用户手册

Part Ⅳ　Practical Writing ‖ 实用写作

【Instruction】

In working scenario, a beauty practitioner will come across practical writing on some particular occasions. In this part, you will study a main form of beauty practical writing—ordering letter.

【Objective】

Know how to write an ordering letter.

Task 5　Ordering Letter
订购函

【Description】

An ordering letter will be sent to the suppliers when you want to place an order of some products, services, and so on.

Structure:

An ordering letter usually consists of three parts:

1. the title(such as Ordering Letter)

2. the body(details like exact product or service, quantity, price, size/type, etc.)

3. the signature(the purchaser)

Example:

Ordering Letter

Dec. 10, 2017

Dear Sir or Madam,

　　Thank you for your letter of Dec. 5 with the illustrated catalogue of your latest products and price list. We are interested in your new type of cosmetic sprayer AW1001. We would like to buy 15 sets of this type and wonder if you could offer a discount on the price. If so, we will go and visit you on Dec. 22. Is it suitable for you? Please inform us as soon as possible.

　　I am looking forward to your reply.

Your faithfully,
Sue

Summarize 项目小结

In this unit we have learnt:

1. How to express processes of skin care.

2. Knowledge about solutions to skin problems and operation introduction of photon skin rejuvenation device.

3. How to write an ordering letter.

Test Yourself 能力检测

1. Read the conversation of Task 2 and mark the statements true(T) or false(F).

____(1)If your skin is dry, you just need to replenish water every day.

____(2)If you have oily skin, you'll have many pimples on your mouth and face.

____(3)Don't eat too much seafood if you have sensitive skin.

____(4)Be cautious to eat spicy food if you have oily skin.

____(5)It's better to have moisturizing masks every day.

2. Choose the proper translation for each sentence based on Task 2.

____(1)We can also simply know our skin type by observing how much oil our skin produces.

____(2)I have oily skin. Just as many young boys and girls, I have many pimples and acne on my forehead and nose.

____(3)Obviously, your skin is sensitive. You ought to be cautious to choose and use soft skin care products and eat less seafood.

____(4)您最好选择清爽的乳液或霜。记得少吃辛辣的食物。

____(5)在任何时候，补水和保湿都是很重要的，对于干性或混合型皮肤的人来说尤其如此，最好每天或至少一周三次使用保湿面膜。

A. 很明显您是敏感性皮肤。您应该谨慎地去选择和使用温和的护肤产品且少吃海产品。

B. 通过观察油脂的分泌情况，我们也能简单地了解皮肤的类型。

C. 我是油性皮肤。正如很多年轻人一样，我的额头和鼻子上有很多小脓包和痤疮。

D. You'd better choose light lotion or cream. Remember to eat less spicy food.

E. It's very important to replenish water and keep moisture at any time, especially for people with dry and mixed skin. It's better to have moisturizing masks daily or at least three times a week.

3. According to Task 3, number the proper process of facial care.

(   )First, I'll give you a makeup removal and select a gentle cleansing lotion to clean your face.

(   )Please take off your coat, necklace and earrings, and put on this gown. Lie down, please.

(　　)After the cleansing stage, I'll have an exfoliation with scrubbing cream for you.

(　　)I'll use the cosmetic sprayer to open your facial pore to let the dirt and the waste out and nutrient into the skin.

(　　)After cleansing and exfoliation, I will massage your face with essential oil for 15-20 minutes and then apply a facial mask.

4. According to Task 4, choose the proper color of the light based on the functions given.

Color	Function
	Neutralize and balance skin condition.
	Enhance the energy uptake by cells gradually, and promote metabolism.
	Heal and repair the acne scar.
	Resolve age spots, and improve fine lines.
	Improve coarseness, wrinkle, redness and fever of the skin, and increase immunity.
	Resist wrinkle, repair damaged skin, and smooth the fine wrinkles.
	Repair the skin without leaving scars.

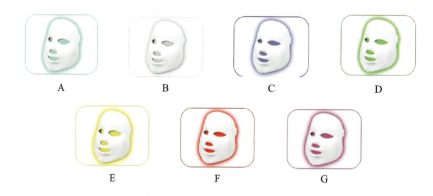

A　　B　　C　　D

E　　F　　G

5. Writing practice based on Task 5.

说明：请先阅读下面这封来信，假设你是信中的 Mrs. Li，请依据信中的内容写一封回信。回信中应包括以下要点：

（1）对来信表示感谢；

（2）对新型 W1070 光子嫩肤仪很感兴趣；

（3）打算购买 120 台光子嫩肤仪，询问对方价格能否降低；

（4）拟于 11 月 25 日前往贵公司看货。

来信：

Nov. 6, 2019

Dear Mrs. Li,

　　I am writing to introduce a new type of photon skin rejuvenation device to you.

It's the latest product and the model is W1070. If you would like to buy it, we would be happy to sell it to you for 2560 yuan each device. That is the cheapest one of the same kinds on sale.

If you are interested in it, please contact me with the above address. Could you suggest a time when you are available to try out the product? I am looking forward to your reply.

Yours truly,
Zhang Hua
Sales Manager

课程思政 Curriculum Ideology and Politics

Xi Jinping's Quotations 习近平语录

要坚持党的领导，坚持正确办学方向，坚持立德树人，优化职业教育类型定位，深化产教融合、校企合作，深入推进育人方式、办学模式、管理体制、保障机制改革，稳步发展职业本科教育，建设一批高水平职业院校和专业，推动职普融通，增强职业教育适应性。

——习近平对职业教育工作作出重要指示
2021 年 4 月 13 日

It is important to adhere to the Party's leadership, follow the correct path of running schools, persist in fostering virtues through education and refine the orientation of vocational education. We should deepen the integration of vocational education with industries, promote cooperation between colleges and businesses and move forward with reform in training and schooling models, as well as management and support mechanisms. Steady progress should be made in developing undergraduate programs for vocational education, building a group of top-notch vocational institutions and programs, promoting the integration between vocational and general education and making vocational education more adaptive.

——Xi Jinping gives important instructions
on vocational education work
Apr. 13, 2021

Key Words and Expressions

follow the correct path of running schools　坚持正确办学方向
deepen the integration of vocational education with industries　深化产教融合
cooperation between colleges and businesses　校企合作
promoting the integration between vocational and general education　推动职普融通

（杨　琴　余芊芊）

Unit 4　Body Care
第四单元　身体护理

图 4-1

 Learning Objectives ┃ 学习目标

1. Master the expressions of head and neck care.
2. Master the expressions of back care.
3. Understand the knowledge of yin-yang and five elements.
4. Know how to write an activity invitation letter.

Part Ⅰ　Listening ‖ 听

【Instruction】

Listening is a basic skill for cosmetology application English. In this part, you will hear a short passage. It will be read twice. For extensive listening, you should be able to understand the outline of the passage. For intensive listening, the key words are important.

【Objectives】

1. First listening: Try to get the main idea of the passage.
2. Second listening: Try to grab the key words.

Task 1　Optoelectronic Beauty Technology
光电美容技术

【Description】

Optoelectronic beauty technology is used more and more widely in the modern beauty industry. Try to understand each bold font and choose a correct word from the **Word Bank** for each blank.

图 4-2

图 4-3

Word Bank

A. light　　B. skin　　C. use　　D. hair　　E. layer

Laser

In the clinic, laser is often used to remove spots, moles, 1._____, etc., using a way that is less traumatic to the 2._____, and the effect is good.

扫码听
音频 1

Photorejuvenation

DPL photorejuvenation uses a specific narrow spectrum of 3. _____, directly irradiated on the surface of the skin. The photons can penetrate deep into the skin and stimulate the proliferation of subcutaneous collagen.

Ultherapy

Ultherapy and 7D polylates 4. _____ high-intensity focused ultrasound, which can reach a temperature of 65-70 ℃ under the skin, stimulating the regeneration and arrangement of collagen in dermal tissue to increase skin elasticity and reduce wrinkles.

Radiofrequency

Thermage uses a radiofrequency method to achieve a thermal 5. _____ in the deep dermis, improving skin firmness. This form of energy generates a heating effect that penetrates the collagen and causes it to contract and be tight.

扫码看答案 1

扫码看翻译 1

Part Ⅱ　Speaking ‖ 说

【Instruction】

Speaking is a core skill in communicating with clients, introducing programs, recommending products, etc. In this part, you will study two conversations about body care.

【Objectives】

1. Master the underlined sentences for head and neck care.
2. Master the underlined sentences for back care.

Task 2　Head and Neck Care
头颈部护理

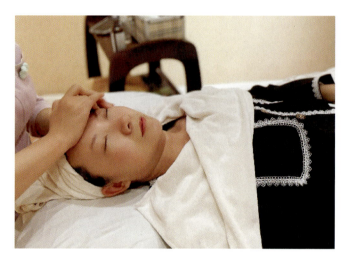

图 4-4

【Description】

A client feels something uneasy with her neck. The beauty adviser is helping her to diagnose the symptoms and introducing the ways to get better.

Think and discuss:

1. What are the causes for neck problem?
2. What is the best treatment for head and neck pain?

图 4-5

Mary—a beauty adviser   Diana Smith—a client

Mary: Mrs. Smith, your complexion becomes better and better now.

Diana Smith: Thanks for your compliment. I keep on applying moisturizing masks every night. But recently I feel a little uncomfortable in my neck and I don't know why.

扫码听音频 2

Mary: Oh, really? Does it hurt when you turn your head?

Diana Smith: It doesn't hurt actually. I just feel something uneasy with my neck. Definitely it's not "stiff neck", because I never sleep over high pillows.

Mary: I see. You probably have too much office work, or you sit at a desk or a computer for too long.

扫码看翻译 2

Diana Smith: That's a bit true. I had loads of business to deal with these days.

Mary: Another thing is tension. In western medicine, doctors believe tension can narrow your blood vessels, which can cause pain or unpleasantness of your body.

Diana Smith: Wow, you are something of a doctor.

Mary: But traditional Chinese medicine holds that any physical problem comes from the unbalance of "Yin" and "Yang". It is also believed that pain arises when the flow of "Qi" is blocked or slowed down. "Yin", "Yang" and "Qi" are common concepts of traditional Chinese medicine.

Diana Smith: What should I do now?

Mary: In order to promote blood circulation and relieve the pain of head and neck, massage is the best treatment. First, the body therapist will use ice lotion to calm the pain and regulate the injured tissue. You'll feel very cool and comfortable at this stage.

Diana Smith: That's interesting. What will happen next?

Mary: Then beautician will massage your head and neck with nourishing lotion, which will revitalize your brain cells, and provide new energy and blood for your head and neck.

Diana Smith: Sounds fantastic! I can't wait to have a try.

Mary: And after the massage, you will sleep better and recover from the tension soon. In addition, this massage program can also help to prevent from losing hair. If you would like to have a try now, Anna is available at the moment.

Diana Smith: How long will it take?

Mary: About an hour. And you will have a 20% discount if you order 10 times from now on.

Diana Smith: OK. I'll take it into consideration if I feel good.

Key Words and Expressions

compliment[ˈkɒmplɪmənt]　n. 赞扬,称赞　v. 赞美,恭维
uneasy[ʌnˈiːzɪ]　adj. 心神不安的,不舒服的
stiff[stɪf]　adj. 僵硬的
vessel[ˈvesl]　n. 血管
tension[ˈtenʃn]　n. 紧张,不安　v. 使紧张,使不安
available[əˈveɪləbl]　adj. 有空的,可获得的
circulation[ˌsɜːkjuːˈleɪʃn]　n. 循环
stiff neck　落枕
take...into consideration　考虑

Task 3　Back Care
背部护理

【Description】

A client feels her back, neck and shoulders are in pain. The beauty adviser is introducing massage, five-element essential oil and capricorn brush to her. The body therapist is using brushing and acupressure to relieve her symptoms.

Think and discuss:

1. Why do many people suffer from pain on some parts of their bodies in summer?

2. Why do black spots appear after brushing?

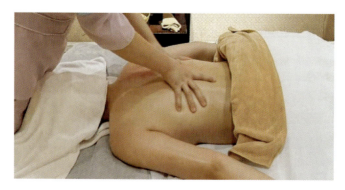

图 4-6

Mary—a beauty adviser   Diana Smith—a client   Sally—a body therapist

Mary: Welcome, Mrs. Smith, how are you recently?

Diana Smith: My back, neck and shoulders are in pain, maybe because the whole summer I had been staying in the air-conditioning room.

Mary: It's natural for many people to suffer from pain on some parts of their bodies staying in an air-conditioning room for too long, because the lack of exercising causes the invasion of coldness, the deficiency of "Qi" and poor blood circulation.

扫码听
音频 3

Diana Smith: How would you relieve my pain?

Mary: Besides massage, we recommend using five-element essential oil and capricorn brush to brush your body, which can improve blood circulation, eliminate "Qi" stagnation and blood stasis, and make you more energetic and healthier.

扫码看
翻译 3

Diana Smith: Let me have a look at the brush. Wow, it's so sharp. Will it hurt my skin?

Mary: No. First, I will try to brush your back. You'll feel a bit pain. Please let me know if you can't stand it.

Diana Smith: Yeah, it really hurts, but I can bear it.

Mary: There are seven reflection areas on a person's back: lung, heart, spleen and stomach, liver and gallbladder, kidney, drainage, and reproduction areas, which is also called Baliao Area. Well, now let's have a back diagnosis to find out some physical problems in sub-health state.

Diana Smith: OK.

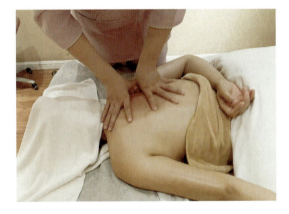

图 4-7

Mary: After brushing your back, it's obvious to see the clots and nodes on your back. And perhaps you have a headache, dizzy and insomnia sometimes.

Diana Smith: Yes, you're right.

Mary: Your liver and gallbladder area is clearly prominent and there are some obvious black spots, which shows the function of your liver is slowing down. As accumulation of toxins develops, you are likely to have constipation.

Diana Smith: I do have constipation, but not often.

Mary: Your kidney area looks a little dark and your pores are visible, which indicates that you are sensitive to cold weather and your legs and feet are prone to get swollen. All of these problems will arise because of the poor circulation of "Qi" and the blood.

Diana Smith: Wow, it sounds magic.

Mary: Now, Sally is serving you.

Sally: Mrs. Smith, I'm very glad to serve you. If you feel intolerable to my brushing or acupressure, please let me know.

Diana Smith: OK. Thank you.

Sally: My pleasure.

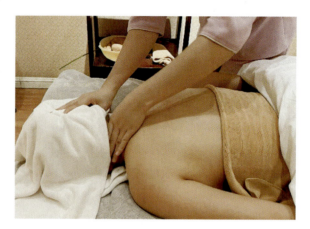

图 4-8

(40 *minutes later, Mary gives some advice to Diana Smith after brushing.*)

Mary: Do you still feel pain now?

Diana Smith: No, I'm refreshed. How long will it takes for the redness on my back to fade away?

Mary: It depends on your own health. In general, it may disappear within one or two hours, but for some weak people, occasionally four or five days.

Diana Smith: Can I have a bath tonight?

Mary: After four hours, the essential oil will be completely absorbed by your skin. So you can have a shower at night. Remember to drink more water or juice.

Diana Smith: Thank you.

Mary: Not at all.

Key Words and Expressions

stagnation[stæɡˈneɪʃn]　n. 停滞
intolerable[ɪnˈtɒlərəbl]　adj. 无法忍受的
diagnosis[ˌdaɪəɡˈnəʊsɪs]　n. 诊断，判断
invasion[ɪnˈveɪʒn]　n. 入侵，侵略
blockage[ˈblɒkɪdʒ]　n. 堵塞
node[nəʊd]　n. 节，瘤，结节
rejuvenate[rɪˈdʒuːvəneɪt]　v. 使……年轻，使……恢复精神
reflection[rɪˈflekʃn]　n. 反射，反映
reproduction[ˌriːprəˈdʌkʃn]　n. 生殖
clot[klɒt]　n. 凝块，堵塞物
dizzy[ˈdɪzi]　adj. 头昏眼花的，使人头晕的
insomnia[ɪnˈsɒmniə]　n. 失眠
constipation[ˌkɒnstɪˈpeɪʃn]　n. 便秘
air-conditioning room　空调房

Part Ⅲ　Reading ‖ 读

【Instruction】

For a beauty practitioner, reading especially extensive reading is a necessary skill. In this part, you will study a text related to body care.

【Objectives】

1. Find the topic sentence for each paragraph.
2. Try to get the main idea of the text.

Task 4　Yin-Yang and Five Elements
阴阳和五行

【Description】

The theories of yin-yang and five elements are ways to better understand the dynamics of human body. They are closely related to body treatment. Yin-yang and five elements must be in balance.

图 4-9

In the ancient oriental medicine system, the theories of yin-yang and five elements are integrated as a way of better understanding the dynamics of human body.

Yin and yang literally mean shadow and light, respectively. Yang energy is considered to be male, hot, dry, bright and active, and it's associated with the sun, daytime and summertime. Yin energy is considered to be female, cool, wet, dark and quiet, and it's associated with the moon, nighttime and wintertime.

As *Huangdi Neijing* (*Inner Canon of Huangdi*) expounds: "Yin and yang serve as the heaven and the earth, the fundamental principle of all things."

图 4-10

The five elements, also called "Wu Xing", are earth, metal, water, wood and fire.

They are fundamental to the cycles of nature, and therefore correspond to the human body. All the five elements must be in balance with each other. If not, signs and symptoms appear and tell us which of the elements may be weak.

图 4-11

Key Words and Expressions

oriental [ˌɔːriˈentl] adj. 东方的，东方人的

dynamics [daɪˈnæmɪks] n. 动力学，动态原理

five elements 五行

associate with 与……相联系

Huangdi Neijing (*Inner Canon of Huangdi*) 《黄帝内经》

be fundamental to 对……很重要

Part Ⅳ　Practical Writing ‖ 实用写作

【Instruction】

In working scenario, a beauty practitioner will come across practical writing on some particular occasions. In this part, you will study a main form of beauty practical writing—activity invitation letter.

【Objective】

Know how to write an activity invitation letter.

图 4-12

Task 5　Activity Invitation Letter
活动邀请函

【Description】

An activity invitation letter will be sent when a well-known person, expert, VIP client, etc. is invited to participate in an activity.

Structure:

An activity invitation letter usually consists of three parts:

1. the title(such as Activity Invitation)

2. the body(details like activity, time, place, etc.)

3. the signature(organizer)

Activity invitation letter format:

Activity Invitation

Dear _____(name of the receiver),

We are very pleased to invite you to attend _____(name of the event) that will be held on _____(date and time of the event), _____(venue of the event).

This event is _____(genre of the event) and looking forward to seeing you in the event. Your presence will make this event even more special and lit.

Thank you.

Yours truly,

_____(name/signature)

Summarize 项目小结

In this unit we have learnt：

1. How to express procedures for head and neck care，and back care.

2. Knowledge about optoelectronic beauty technology，and yin-yang and five elements.

3. How to write an activity invitation letter.

Test Yourself 能力检测

1. Match each English word or expression in Column A with its Chinese meaning in Column B based on Task 2.

Column A	Column B
(1) massage	A. 疼痛
(2) pain	B. 按摩
(3) blood circulation	C. 血液循环
(4) uncomfortable	D. 保湿
(5) moisturizing	E. 有空的,可获得的
(6) discount	F. 落枕
(7) available	G. 面色,肤色
(8) complexion	H. 循环
(9) circulation	I. 折扣
(10) stiff neck	J. 不舒服的

扫码看答案 2

2. Choose the best answer based on Task 2.

____(1) Mrs. Smith's complexion becomes better and better because _____.

A. she is young

B. Mary did facial care for her every week

C. she uses moisturizing masks every night

D. she sleeps well recently

____(2) Mrs. Smith feels uneasy with her _____.

A. neck   B. back   C. leg   D. head

____(3) In western medicine, doctors believe tension can narrow your _____.

A. nerves   B. blood vessels   C. cells   D. mind

_____(4) Diana Smith has _____ business to deal with these days.

A. a few　　　　B. little　　　　C. loads of　　　　D. some

_____(5) Traditional Chinese medicine holds that any physical problem comes from the _____ of "Yin" and "Yang".

A. inner　　　　B. balance　　　　C. unbalance　　　　D. form

_____(6) In order to promote blood circulation and relieve the pain of head and neck, _____ is the best treatment.

A. massage　　　　B. medicine　　　　C. acupuncture　　　　D. manicure

_____(7) "Yin", "Yang" and "Qi" are common _____ of traditional Chinese medicine.

A. ways　　　　B. consideration　　　　C. times　　　　D. concepts

_____(8) After the massage, one will sleep better and _____ from the tension soon.

A. recover　　　　B. escape　　　　C. suffer　　　　D. take

_____(9) If Mrs. Smith would like to have a try now, Anna is _____ at the moment.

A. afraid　　　　B. agree　　　　C. available　　　　D. astute

_____(10) Mrs. Smith will have a 20% _____ if she orders 10 times from now on.

A. service　　　　B. discount　　　　C. moment　　　　D. try

3. Decide whether the statement is true(T) or false(F) based on Task 3.

_____(1) Staying in the air-conditioning room for too long will cause pain in your body.

_____(2) Five-element essential oil and capricorn brush can improve blood circulation.

_____(3) The brush is so sharp that it will hurt your skin.

_____(4) There are eight reflecting areas on your back.

_____(5) Having a back diagnosis can find out some physical problems in sub-health state.

_____(6) If your circulation is blocked severely, we'll see some brushed parts become red and purple.

_____(7) You feel headache, dizzy and insomnia, which shows you have troubles in your neck and back.

_____(8) There're some black spots on your liver part, which shows the function of your liver is normal.

_____(9) The redness on the back will fade away in one day.

____(10) You can take a shower two hours after back care.

4. Match each picture with the proper back care equipment based on Task 3.

(1) massage bed _____

(2) capricorn brush _____

(3) massage oil _____

(4) towel _____

(5) scraping plate _____

(6) rolling stick _____

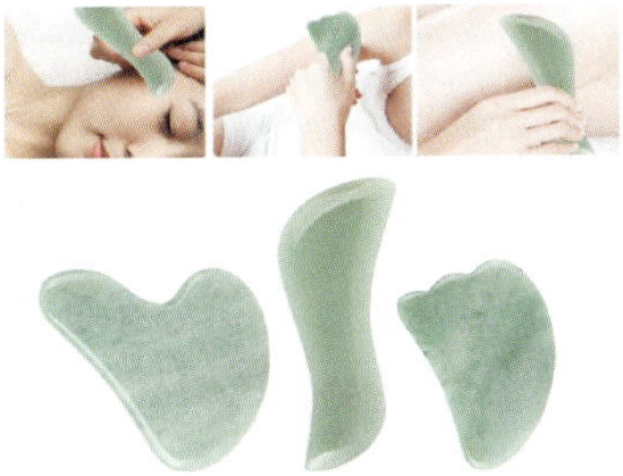

图 4-13(选项 A)

图 4-14(选项 B)

图 4-15(选项 C)

图 4-16(选项 D)

图 4-17(选项 E)

图 4-18(选项 F)

5. Choose the proper translation for each phrase based on Task 4.

(1) _____ ancient oriental medicine system

(2) _____ fundamental principle

(3) _____ 五行

(4) _____ 阴阳理论

(5) _____ 与人体相对应

A. 古代东方医学体系

B. 基本原则

C. correspond to the human body

D. the theory of yin and yang

E. five elements

6. Writing practice based on Task 5.

说明：假设你是爱美丽美容院的工作人员，美容院将于5月21日星期六上午10:00在兴达广场一楼举办10周年庆典，届时将有回馈活动和礼品，欢迎新老顾客参加。请用英语写一则活动邀请函。

课程思政 Curriculum Ideology and Politics

Xi Jinping's Quotations 习近平语录

技术工人队伍是支撑中国制造、中国创造的重要力量。……希望广大参赛选手奋勇拼搏、争创佳绩，展现新时代技能人才的风采。各级党委和政府要高度重视技能人才工作，大力弘扬劳模精神、劳动精神、工匠精神，激励更多劳动者特别是青年一代走技能成才、技能报国之路，培养更多高技能人才和大国工匠，为全面建设社会主义现代化国家提供有力人才保障。

——选自"习近平致首届全国职业技能大赛的贺信"

2020年12月10日

Technical workers are main forces underpinning made-in-China and created-in-China sector and innovation drive... Hope the participants will strive for good results, show the demeanor of skilled talents in the new era. All levels of government should attach more importance to training skilled workers and make efforts to carry forward the spirit of model workers, labor and craftsmanship, stimulate more workers, especially the younger generation, to improve their skills, and foster more highly skilled workers

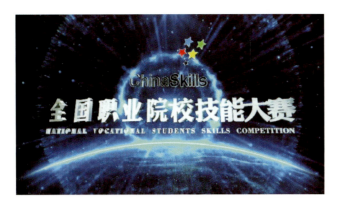

图 4-19

and craftsmen in a bid to achieve the goal of fully building a modern socialist country.

——Selected from "Xi Jinping's Congratulatory Letter to the Country's First Vocational Skills Competition"

Dec. 10, 2020

Key Words and Expressions

vocational skills competition　职业技能大赛
the spirit of craftsmanship　工匠精神
new era　新时代

（崔　宁　余芊芊）

Unit 5 Color Cosmetics and Cosmetician
第五单元 彩妆产品和化妆师

图 5-1

Learning Objectives 　学习目标

1. Master the expressions of cosmetics brand.
2. Master the expressions of daily makeup and bridal makeup.
3. Understand the current situation of the color cosmetics market in China.
4. Know how to write a resume.

Part Ⅰ　Listening 　听

【Instruction】

Listening is a basic skill for cosmetology application English. In this part, you

will hear a short passage. It will be read twice. For extensive listening, you should be able to understand the outline of the passage. For intensive listening, the key words are important.

【Objectives】

1. First listening: Try to get the main idea of the passage.
2. Second listening: Try to grab the key words.

Task 1　Cosmetics Brand
彩妆品牌

【Description】

When it comes to cosmetics, quality matters. How can we talk about fantastic cosmetics brands without mentioning the following ones? Try to understand each bold font and choose a correct word from the **Word Bank** for each blank.

图 5-2

图 5-3

Word Bank

A. professional　　B. signature　　C. industry　　D. family-owned　　E. incredible

It is not easy to rate top cosmetics brands, as one brand can have better foundation while the other one can beat the same brand through lipstick. We have compiled a list of some better cosmetics brands in the world at the moment.

扫码听
音频 1

Chanel

Let's start with a cosmetics brand you've probably heard of, and even if you haven't, Chanel's cosmetics are 1._____. The products are expensive, but they are well worth it. Chanel's cosmetics are recognized for their exceptional quality and innovative compositions.

MAC

Make-up Art Cosmetics (MAC) is the world's giant cosmetics and beauty company. The company initially launched products only for 2. _____ cosmetics artists but are now available for consumers directly. The quality of MAC's cosmetics is unbeatable and the products are expensive just as most qualitative cosmetic products are.

Dior

If you haven't yet tried any of their cosmetic products, you are truly missing out. Without a doubt, their Dior Addict Lipstick is their 3. _____ , and it is probably the best-selling lipstick in the world.

L'Oreal

As a global leader, L'Oreal is a trendsetter in the beauty 4. _____ and has been for decades. This French cosmetics company has brought us some of the most popular mascara, eyeliner, foundations and lip care in the world.

Maybelline

Almost everyone has heard of Maybelline. Maybelline has started off as a small 5. _____ business, but it has expanded into one of the largest cosmetics brands in the US.

扫码看答案 1

扫码看翻译 1

Part Ⅱ　Speaking ‖ 说

【Instruction】

Speaking is a core skill in communicating with clients, introducing programs, recommending products, etc. In this part, you will study two conversations about makeup.

【Objectives】

1. Master the underlined sentences for daily makeup.

2. Master the underlined sentences for bridal makeup.

Task 2　Process of Daily Makeup
日常妆步骤

图 5-4

【Description】

The cosmetician is explaining makeup knowledge to a client and helping her create natural and beautiful makeup effects.

Think and discuss:

1. How many types of UV protector are there?

2. What is the secret to permanently possess the magical effects of makeup?

图 5-5

图 5-6

Amy—a client　Betty—a cosmetician

Amy: Betty, you look pretty well!

Betty: Thank you. You look good too. No matter where I go, I wear makeup. You know makeup is really amazing. It can embellish

扫码听
音频 2

your complexion and facial features. It can make you look even more beautiful.

Amy：Yeah, as the saying goes, "Nobody is not in love with beauty." Maybe you will feel better after finishing your makeup, but some people treat their faces as plates and put on all kinds of colors. I think that's terrible.

扫码看翻译2

Betty：That's probably due to their lacking of professional knowledge. In fact, real makeup is to enhance natural beauty. Therefore, the best natural makeup should be as if there's no makeup. It is also called nude makeup.

Amy：Right, but how to get that natural effect?

Betty：First, you should always do basic skin care so that your skin won't be hurt. After that, you can use concealer and foundation to conceal facial defects, improving the look of your skin and even modify your facial features. No matter whether the shape of your face is square, round or triangle, proper foundation will make you look good.

图 5-7

Amy：Oh! That's why you look so great.

Betty：Right.

Amy：It is said that UV protector is divided into purple and green UV protectors. What color UV protector should I choose?

Betty：Your complexion is yellow and gloomy. I think purple UV protector will suit you and make your skin whiter. Green UV protector is suitable to the skin in red.

Amy：After that, what else should I do?

Betty：After the makeup base, you should prune your eyebrows and pencil the eyebrows. Your eyebrows are dense, but they have no three-dimensional effect because of odd hairs. And since your hair is black, you can extend the end of your eyebrow with black eyebrow powder and make it have more three-dimensional effect.

Amy：Yes. I am all ears.

Betty：There follows the part of eye makeup. Firstly, wear eye shadows in three similar colors and then wear eye liner and mascara. Your eyelashes are a bit long, but not very thick and curly, so I suggest you curl your eyelashes, and then use L'Oreal Paris double extension mascara to make your eyes bigger and more beautiful.

Amy：Have I finished my daily makeup after these processes?

Betty: No, after the eye makeup, you can apply blush compact and lipstick which can embellish your complexion and facial features.

Amy: Wow! It sounds like a lot of fun. Are these all the secrets to your perfect makeup?

图 5-8

Betty: Well, the most crucial and final work is to remove your final makeup thoroughly. That's the secret to permanently possess the magical effects of makeup.

Amy: I see. Thank you very much!

Betty: You are welcome.

Key Words and Expressions

embellish[ɪmˈbelɪʃ]　v. 美化,装饰,修饰
enhance[ɪnˈhɑːns]　v. 提高,增加,加强
foundation[faʊnˈdeɪʃn]　n. 粉底
defect[ˈdiːfekt]　n. 瑕疵,毛病
modify[ˈmɒdɪfaɪ]　v. 修饰,修改
triangle[ˈtraɪæŋgl]　n. 三角形
gloomy[ˈgluːmɪ]　adj. 暗淡的,阴暗的
mascara[mæˈskɑːrə]　n. 睫毛膏
lipstick[ˈlɪpstɪk]　n. 口红
crucial[ˈkruːʃl]　adj. 关键的,决定性的
permanently[ˈpɜːmənəntlɪ]　adv. 永久地
magical[ˈmædʒɪkl]　adj. 神奇的,奇妙的
eye shadow　眼影
blush compact　腮红

Task 3 Tips of Bridal Makeup
新娘化妆小贴士

【Description】

A client is getting married. The cosmetician is making beautiful bridal makeup for her based on her facial features and skin type, and giving her some tips in case of emergency.

Think and discuss:

1. Why do people smear UV protector before they make up?
2. What advice does the cosmetician give to the bride after putting on makeup?

图 5-9

Mary—a beauty receptionist   Helen—a client   Jimmy—a cosmetician

Mary: Good afternoon, what can I do for you?

Helen: I'm getting married. <u>Can you arrange an experienced makeup artist for me</u>?

Mary: Sure. This is Jimmy, our best cosmetician. This is Helen, she wants to make bridal makeup.

Jimmy: Hello, Helen.

Helen: Hello, Jimmy. Can you help me?

Jimmy: Of course, <u>on the wedding day, the bride should be the most beautiful lady and I'm sure to make you the shinning focus on that day.</u>

Helen: Really?

Jimmy: Believe me. Since you need heavy and beautiful makeup, we should use cosmetics that can last a long time so that you will look best in photography. Firstly, let me see your facial features and your skin type. I'll choose proper makeup for you.

Helen: OK.

Jimmy: Well, you have a round face and mixed skin. The T-zone is oily and the cheeks are a bit dry. All right, let me clean your skin first.

Helen: Thank you. Mm, what did you spray just now?

图 5-10

Jimmy: I just sprayed silk whitening lotion and smeared nourishing cream, and then I will prune your eyebrows. Your eyebrows are dense, but they have no three-dimensional effect because of the strays. Please raise your head. OK, thanks. I will smear UV protector before I make up.

Helen: Why should I smear UV protector?

Jimmy: Because cosmetics will hurt our skin. What kind of wedding dress will you choose?

Helen: I'd like to choose an open-neckline wedding dress.

Jimmy: Well, if your dress has an open neckline, I will sweep your neck and chest with a thin layer of bronzing powder to make them appear a warm color. I'll give you some tips: carry a touch-up kit with concealer, powder, lipstick or transparent lipstick, lip line pencil and tissue paper. Also, prepare a mini sewing kit for sewing clothes in case of emergency. They will be helpful. All right, your bridal makeup is finished.

Helen: Great! Thanks a lot.

Jimmy: My pleasure.

图 5-11

Key Words and Expressions

wedding['wedɪŋ]　n. 婚礼,结婚庆典
bride[braɪd]　n. 新娘
focus['fəʊkəs]　n. 焦点,中心　v. 聚焦,调整
spray[spreɪ]　v. 喷,喷射　n. 喷雾,喷雾器
smear[smɪə]　v. 涂抹,敷
neckline['neklaɪn]　n. 领口
tissue['tɪʃuː]　n. 纸巾
sewing['səʊɪŋ]　n. 缝纫,缝制物
kit[kɪt]　n. 成套工具,工具箱
emergency[ɪ'mɜːdʒənsɪ]　n. 突发事件,紧急状态
touch-up kit　补妆包
sewing kit　针线包

Part Ⅲ　Reading ‖ 读

【Instruction】

For a beauty practitioner, reading especially extensive reading is a necessary skill. In this part, you will study a text related to the color cosmetics market in China.

【Objectives】

1. Find the topic sentence for each paragraph.
2. Try to get the main idea of the text.

Task 4 Color Cosmetics Market in China
中国彩妆市场

【Description】

Women need cosmetics now more than ever. Just the act of applying cosmetics can lift up their spirits and give them a different outlook on life.

图 5-12

Cosmetics cover a wide range of products used for cleaning, grooming, and beautifying the face and body. Various cosmetic products sold in China include color cosmetics, skincare products, hair care products, and toiletries. With more and more international colored cosmetics brands entering the domestic market, the beauty and cosmetics industry will be one of the fastest-growing and most promising fields of business in China.

扫码听音频 4

The two categories that are most concerned about in the cosmetics market are skincare products and color cosmetics. According to statistics, Chinese cosmetics market accounted for about half of the Asia-Pacific cosmetics market and more than one fifth of the world cosmetics market in 2021. Currently, skincare

扫码看翻译 4

products dominate the Chinese cosmetics market. A Chinese consumer spends an average of 210 yuan on skincare products every year, approximately four fifths of the total cosmetics spending. As the second largest cosmetics market in the world, China's color cosmetics market is also very promising.

图 5-13

The beauty industry has witnessed a wave of innovations in recent years. Color cosmetics with Chinese characteristics are becoming increasingly popular. Three of the ten most successful cosmetics companies in China in 2021 were local companies. In 2020, Perfect Diary, a Chinese cosmetics company, surpassed Dior to take the second-largest position in the Chinese cosmetics market.

图 5-14

Key Words and Expressions

grooming [ˈɡruːmɪŋ] n. 打扮，装束
toiletry [ˈtɔɪlətrɪ] n. 洗漱用品

domestic[dəˈmestɪk]   adj. 国内的，家庭的
category[ˈkætəgərɪ]   n. 类别
dominate[ˈdɒmɪneɪt]   v. 支配，控制，(在比赛中)占有优势，占据主动
approximately[əˈprɒksɪmətlɪ]   adv. 大约，大概
innovation[ˌɪnəˈveɪʃn]   n. 改革，创新
characteristic[ˌkærəktəˈrɪstɪk]   n. 特点，特征，品质
surpass[səˈpɑːs]   v. 超过，超越
Asia-Pacific   亚太地区
be concerned about   关注
account for   （数量或比例上）占，导致

Part Ⅳ　Practical Writing ‖ 实用写作

【Instruction】

In working scenario, a beauty practitioner will come across practical writing on some particular occasions. In this part, you will study a main form of beauty practical writing—resume.

【Objective】

Know how to write a resume.

Task 5　Resume
简历

【Description】

A resume is a personal profile provided by a job seeker to the employer. For job seekers, clear and distinctive resumes can help them stand out among numerous competitors.

Structure：

A resume usually consists of the following parts：

1. personal information
2. work experience

3. awards

4. skills

5. self-evaluation

More information can be added if needed.

图 5-15

Example:

Resume

Personal Information:

Name: Li Mei

Gender: Female

Date of Birth: August 18, 2002

Contact Number: 130-××××-××××

E-mail: 123456@qq.com

Major: Medical beauty technology

Work Experience:

I worked as a tutor for senior middle school students.

Awards:

National Scholarship, merit student, outstanding student cadre

Skills:

Language: English(fluent)

Computer: Proficient in using PowerPoint, Excel, and Word

Self-evaluation:

I'm a motivated and independent girl with a passion for continuous growth and learning. I adapt quickly to challenges, and I have great problem-solving abilities.

Summarize 项目小结

In this unit we have learnt:

1. How to express procedures for daily makeup and bridal makeup.

2. Knowledge about the current situation of the color cosmetics market in China.

3. How to write a resume.

Test Yourself 能力检测

1. Match each English word or expression in Column A with its Chinese meaning in Column B based on Task 2.

Column A	Column B
(1) modify	A. 提高,增加
(2) embellish	B. 暗淡的
(3) foundation	C. 美化,装饰保湿
(4) enhance	D. 修饰,修改
(5) gloomy	E. 粉底
(6) defect	F. 三角形
(7) UV protector	G. 瑕疵,毛病
(8) triangle	H. 隔离霜
(9) permanently	I. 关键的,决定性的
(10) crucial	J. 永久地

扫码看答案 2

2. Decide whether the statement is true(T) or false(F) based on Task 2.

　　____(1) If you want to look nice, you should put all kinds of color on your face.

　　____(2) The best makeup should look natural, as if there's no makeup.

　　____(3) You'd better do some skincare before makeup so that you'll look nice.

　　____(4) If your face is square, you'll look terrible after making up.

　　____(5) The secret of successful makeup is to remove your makeup thoroughly before sleeping.

　　____(6) A green UV protector is suitable for Betty's skin.

　　____(7) The first step in makeup is to prune your eyebrows and pencil the eyebrows.

　　____(8) Heavy and beautiful makeup will enhance natural beauty.

　　____(9) You can use concealer and foundation to conceal facial defects.

　　____(10) If you want your eyebrows to be more three-dimensional, you can use an eyebrow pencil that matches the color of your hair.

3. Match each picture with the proper cosmetic accessories based on Task 3.

(1) sponge _____

(2) eyebrow knife _____

(3) lip brush _____

(4) powder puff _____

(5) eyelash curler _____

(6) blush brush _____

图 5-16(选项 A)

图 5-17(选项 B)

图 5-18(选项 C)

图 5-19(选项 D)

图 5-20(选项 E)

图 5-21(选项 F)

4. Decide whether the statement is true(T) or false(F) based on Task 3.

____ (1) Helen wants the receptionist to do daily makeup for her.

____ (2) Jimmy is an experienced makeup artist.

____ (3) Helen's eyebrows aren't very nice because of the strays.

____ (4) Helen's eyebrows are dense, and they have a three-dimensional effect.

____ (5) Jimmy suggests that Helen should carry a touch-up kit and a sewing kit.

____ (6) Helen has a square face and mixed skin.

____ (7) Jimmy advises Helen to bring silk whitening lotion, lipstick or transparent lipstick, lip liner and tissue.

____(8) Helen needs the best natural makeup, so that she will look the best in photography.

____(9) We should smear UV protector before makeup, because cosmetics will hurt our skin.

____(10) It is difficult for Helen to decide which dress to wear.

5. Choose the proper translation for each phrase based on Task 4.

(1)_____ the beauty and cosmetics industry

(2)_____ skincare products

(3)_____ 彩妆市场

(4)_____ 增长最快、最有前途的商业领域

(5)_____ 占据第二位

A. 护肤品

B. 美容和化妆品行业

C. take the second-largest position

D. color cosmetics market

E. the fastest-growing and most promising fields of business

6. Writing practice based on Task 5.

说明：假设你是一名准备找工作的美容相关专业毕业生，请依照自己的实际情况用英语写一份简历。

课程思政 Curriculum Ideology and Politics

Xi Jinping's Quotations 习近平语录

技术工人队伍是支撑中国制造、中国创造的重要基础，对推动经济高质量发展具有重要作用。要健全技能人才培养、使用、评价、激励制度，大力发展技工教育，大规模开展职业技能培训，加快培养大批高素质劳动者和技术技能人才。要在全社会弘扬精益求精的工匠精神，激励广大青年走技能成才、技能报国之路。

——选自"习近平对我国选手在世界技能大赛取得佳绩作出重要指示"

2019 年 9 月 23 日

Technical workers serve as an important foundation supporting made-in-China and created-in-China, and play a key role in high-quality economic growth. More efforts should be made to improve the system for training, employing, evaluating and motivating skilled workers, develop technical education, carry out vocational training on a large scale, and accelerate the training of a large number of high-quality workers and skilled technical personnel. In the whole society, we should carry forward craftsmanship spirit with the pursuit of excellence, and encourage young people to develop their skills to serve the country.

——Selected from "Xi Jinping made the remarks in a written instruction to congratulate Chinese contestants on their good results at the 45th WorldSkills Competition"

September 23, 2019

Key Words and Expressions

made-in-China   中国制造
created-in-China   中国创造
high-quality economic growth   经济高质量发展
technical education   技工教育
vocational training   职业技能培训

（刘　颖　余芊芊）

Unit 6　Manicure
第六单元　美甲

图 6-1

扫码看 PPT

Learning Objectives ｜ 学习目标

1. Master the expressions of getting a manicure.
2. Master the expressions of the process of manicure.
3. Understand the promising future of the manicure industry.
4. Know how to write a work schedule.

Part Ⅰ　Listening ‖ 听

【Instruction】

　　Listening is a basic skill for cosmetology application English. In this part, you will hear a short passage. It will be read twice. For extensive listening, you should be able to understand the outline of the passage. For intensive listening, the key words are important.

【Objectives】

1. First listening: Try to get the main idea of the passage.
2. Second listening: Try to grab the key words.

Task 1　The Job of a Manicurist
　　　　美甲师的工作

【Description】

Beautiful and natural nails require care and proper manicuring. By listening to the passage, get to know about the job of a manicurist. Try to choose a correct word from the **Word Bank** for each blank.

图 6-2

图 6-3

> **Word Bank**
> A. advice　　B. sterilize　　C. communication　　D. technical　　E. clients

The job of a manicurist is to take care of a person's nails, including trimming, shaping, and polishing them. Manicurists also provide hand and foot massages, apply artificial nails, and offer 1._____ on nail care.

扫码听音频 1

Manicurists work in a variety of settings, including nail salons, spas, and beauty salons. They often work with a wide range of 2._____, from regular clients who come in for routine nail maintenance to individuals preparing for special occasions like weddings or proms.

One of the primary responsibilities of manicurists is to maintain the cleanliness and hygiene of their workspace. They must 3. _____ their tools and equipment between each client to prevent the spread of infections and diseases. Manicurists also need to keep up with the latest trends and techniques in nail care, as clients often seek their guidance on fashionable nail designs and colors.

To perform their jobs effectively, manicurists need to have excellent manual dexterity and attention to detail. They must also be skilled at shaping nails and applying polish smoothly and evenly. Additionally, they should have good 4. _____ skills to establish rapport with clients and understand clients' preferences and expectations.

Some manicurists specialize in applying artificial nails, such as acrylic or gel nails. This process involves applying a nail extension and then shaping and polishing it to create a natural-looking result. Manicurists who offer this service must have advanced skills and knowledge in nail enhancements.

Overall, the job of a manicurist requires a combination of 5. _____ skills, creativity, and a client-oriented approach. Manicurists play crucial roles in maintaining the beauty and health of their clients' nails, as well as providing a relaxing and enjoyable experience.

扫码看答案 1

扫码看翻译 1

Part Ⅱ Speaking ‖ 说

【Instruction】

Speaking is a core skill in communicating with clients, introducing programs, recommending products, etc. In this part, you will study two conversations about manicures.

【Objectives】

1. Master the underlined sentences for getting a manicure.
2. Master the underlined sentences for the process of manicure.

Task 2　Getting a Manicure
预约美甲

【Description】

A client is calling to make an appointment for a manicure. The receptionist is negotiating a date and time with her and learning about her special requirements.

Think and discuss:

1. What date and time is set for the appointment?

2. Are there any specific requirements the client would like for the coming manicure?

图 6-4

图 6-5

Mary—a receptionist　　Jennifer—a client

Jennifer: Hi, I would like to make an appointment for a manicure, please.

Mary: Of course, what date and time are you looking for?

Jennifer: How about this Saturday at 11:00 am?

Mary: I'm sorry, we are fully booked on Saturday. Would Sunday work for you?

Jennifer: Yes, Sunday is fine. What time slots do you have?

Mary: We have a vacancy at 1:00 pm or 3:00 pm on Sunday.

扫码听
音频 2

Jennifer: I'll take the 3:00 pm slot, please.

Mary: Great! May I have your name, please?

Jennifer: My name is Jennifer Smith.

Mary: Thank you, Jennifer. Can I also get your phone number in case we need to reach you?

扫码看翻译 2

Jennifer: Sure, my phone number is 001-626-202-3379.

Mary: Perfect, Jennifer. Your appointment for a manicure has been scheduled on Sunday at 3:00 pm. Do you have any special requirements for your manicure?

Jennifer: Just a regular manicure, please.

Mary: Noted. We'll see you on Sunday at 3:00 pm for your regular manicure. Have a great day!

Jennifer: Thank you. You too!

图 6-6

Key Words and Expressions

appointment[əˈpɔɪntmənt]　n. 约会,预约,约定

book[bʊk]　v. 预订,预约

vacancy[ˈveɪkənsɪ]　n. 空处,空位

schedule[ˈskedʒuːl]　v. 为……安排时间,安排,排定

time slot　时段

in case　以防万一

Task 3 Process of Manicure
美甲

【Description】

A client comes for a manicure. The manicurist is communicating with her to know about her preference for design, color and shape, and then doing a manicure according to the client's requirements.

Think and discuss:

1. What kind of design or color is the client looking for today?

2. How long will the entire process take?

图 6-7

图 6-8

Helen—a manicurist   Jennifer—a client

Jennifer: Hello, I have an appointment for a manicure today.

Helen: Hi there! Welcome to our salon. Please have a seat and let's get started. What kind of design or color are you looking for today?

扫码听
音频 3

Jennifer: I would like a French manicure with a hint of glitter on the tips, please.

Helen: Great choice! We can definitely do that for you. Let me prepare your nails first by filing and shaping them. Is there a specific shape you prefer?

Jennifer: I usually go for a square shape, but this time can we try a round shape?

Helen: Of course, we can do a round shape for you. Now, I'll gently push back your cuticles and remove any excess skin around the nail beds.

扫码看
翻译 3

Jennifer: Sounds good! I would also like to have a moisturizing hand massage during the process if possible.

Helen: Absolutely! We offer a relaxing hand massage during the process of manicure. It will leave your hands soft and nourished. Once your cuticles are done, I'll apply a base coat to protect your natural nails.

Jennifer: That's perfect. Is it possible to add some subtle nail art as well? Maybe a small floral design?

Helen: Definitely! We offer a variety of nail art options. We can certainly create a lovely floral design for you. After the base coat, I'll apply the French tip polish and add a touch of glitter as you request.

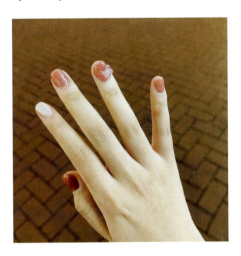

图 6-9

Jennifer: Thank you so much! I'm really excited about this. Will there be any drying time before the final topcoat?

Helen: Yes, after applying the French tips and glitter, we will leave some time for the nails to dry. Once they are completely dry, I'll finish with a clear topcoat to seal everything in and give your nails a glossy finish.

Jennifer: Wonderful! I can't wait to see the final result. How long will the entire process take?

Helen: The whole manicure process, including drying time, usually takes about an hour. But don't worry, we'll make sure it's a relaxing and enjoyable experience for you.

Jennifer: That sounds perfect. Thank you for explaining everything. I'm really looking forward to my new French manicure with a hint of glitter and a floral design.

Helen: You're very welcome! We aim to provide the best service. Please sit back, relax, and let's make your nails shine!

Key Words and Expressions

glitter['glɪtə(r)]　n. 闪烁，闪耀，闪光
file[faɪl]　v. 锉平，锉光滑，锉去
cuticle['kju:tɪkl]　n.（指甲或趾甲根部的）角质层
nourished['nʌrɪʃt]　adj. 滋养的
floral['flɔ:rəl]　adj. 用花制作的，饰以花卉图案的
option['ɒpʃn]　n. 选择，选项，选择权
seal[si:l]　v. 封，密封
glossy['glɒsi]　adj. 平滑有光泽的
nail polish　指甲油
a hint of　一丝
on the tip　在尖端

Part Ⅲ　Reading ‖ 读

【Instruction】

For a beauty practitioner, reading especially extensive reading is a necessary skill. In this part, you will study a text related to the promising future of the manicure industry.

【Objectives】

1. Find the topic sentence for each paragraph.
2. Try to get the main idea of the text.

Task 4 Promising Future of Manicure Industry
美甲行业前景

【Description】

The future of the manicure industry looks exceptionally promising, driven by some factors, which will be illustrated in the following text. With an increasing number of individuals embracing manicure care as part of their self-care routine, it is safe to say that the manicure industry will continue to flourish in the years to come.

图 6-10

The manicure industry has experienced significant growth over the past decade, with an increasing number of individuals seeking professional manicure services. This surge in demand has created a promising future for the manicure industry, offering numerous opportunities for both manicure technicians and entrepreneurs. In this text, we will explore the reasons behind the flourishing manicure industry and its potential for sustainable growth.

扫码听音频 4

Rising Demand

One of the primary factors contributing to the promising future of the manicure industry is the growing demand for professional manicure services. Not only are more women opting for regular manicures and pedicures, but men are also embracing the trend. Additionally, special occasions, such as weddings and parties, often prompt individuals to seek nail enhancements and unique nail art designs.

扫码看
翻译 4

Diversification of Services

The manicure industry has evolved significantly from basic manicures and pedicures. Today, it offers a wide range of services, including gel and acrylic nail extensions, nail art, nail enhancements, and even spa-like treatments for hands and feet. This diversification has attracted a larger customer base, encouraging them to try new and innovative manicure services.

Social Media Influence

Another factor contributing to the rapid growth of the manicure industry is the influence of social media platforms. Manicure technicians and salons now showcase their work on Instagram, Facebook and Pinterest, allowing potential clients to browse through various nail designs and styles. This exposure has increased awareness and curiosity, driving more customers to salons for professional manicure services.

New Technological Advancements

The manicure industry has not been left behind by technological advancements. Innovations such as LED and UV nail lamps for faster drying, gel polishes with longer-lasting effects, and electric nail files have revolutionized the industry. These tools and products have improved both the efficiency and quality of manicure services, attracting more customers who value convenience and durability.

Entrepreneurial Opportunities

The growth of the manicure industry has also created opportunities for aspiring entrepreneurs. Opening a manicure salon or starting a mobile manicure service has become a popular business venture. With the demand for professional manicure services on the rise, individuals with excellent manicure skills and business acumen can establish successful ventures in this industry.

图 6-11

Key Words and Expressions

surge[sɜːdʒ]　n. 陡增，剧增，急剧上升
flourishing[ˈflʌrɪʃɪŋ]　adj. 茁壮成长的，繁荣的，蓬勃发展的
evolve[ɪˈvɒlv]　v. (使)逐步发展，(使)逐渐形成
pedicure[ˈpedɪkjʊə(r)]　n. 美足，足部保养
prompt[prɒmpt]　v. 引起，导致，激起
diversification[daɪˌvɜːsɪfɪˈkeɪʃn]　n. 多样化
showcase[ˈʃəʊkeɪs]　v. 展示……的优点，充分展示
durability[ˌdjʊərəˈbɪləti]　n. 耐用性，持久性
venture[ˈventʃə(r)]　n. (有风险的)企业，投机活动，商业冒险
acumen[ˈækjəmən]　n. 敏锐，精明
opt for　选择
gel and acrylic nail extensions　凝胶和丙烯酸延伸甲

Part Ⅳ　Practical Writing ‖ 实用写作

【Instruction】

In the working scenario, a beauty practitioner will come across practical writing on some particular occasions. In this part, you will study a main form of beauty practical writing—work schedule.

【Objective】

Know how to write a work schedule.

Task 5　Work Schedule
工作计划表

【Description】

A work schedule is to reflect the content of the work plan in the form of a table. Tables are tools for work planning. Through it, the indicators of the work plan or the work items to be completed are listed and summarized, and the basic content of the enterprise work plan is expressed.

Structure:

A work schedule usually consists of three parts:

1. the title(such as Work Schedule)

2. the body(details like task, time, person, etc.)

3. the signature(person who completed the work)

Example:

Weekly Work Schedule

Week Beginning:　　　　　　　　　Your Company:

Dept				Name		
Week	Task	Target	Current	Reasons for Delayed	Measures to be Taken	Remarks
Mon.						
Tues.						
Wed.						
Thurs.						
Fri.						
Sat.						
Sun.						

Summarize 项目小结

In this unit we have learnt：

1. How to make an appointment for a manicure.

2. Knowledge about the process of manicure.

3. Knowledge about the promising future of the manicure industry.

4. How to write a work schedule.

Test Yourself 能力检测

1. Match each English word or expression in Column A with its Chinese meaning in Column B based on Task 2.

Column A	Column B
(1) appointment	A. 空处,空位
(2) vacancy	B. 以防万一
(3) schedule	C. 时段
(4) time slot	D. 为……安排时间,安排,排定
(5) in case	E. 约会,预约,约定

扫码看答案 2

2. Choose the best answer based on Task 2.

____(1) Jennifer would like to make an appointment for a _____.
A. manicure　　B. SPA　　C. body care　　D. facial care

____(2) What date and time are you _____ for?
A. caring　　B. waiting　　C. looking　　D. thinking

____(3) Mary's shop is fully _____ on Saturday.
A. closed　　B. messed　　C. booked　　D. welcomed

____(4) Sunday would _____ for Jennifer.
A. OK　　B. fine　　C. sure　　D. work

____(5) We have a _____ at 1:00 pm or 3:00 pm on Sunday.
A. customer　　B. vacancy　　C. appointment　　D. deal

____(6) Jennifer will take the 3:00 pm time _____.
A. table　　B. slot　　C. plan　　D. slogan

____(7) Can I also get your phone number _____ we need to reach you?
A. in case　　B. even if　　C. for certain　　D. because of

_____(8) Your appointment for a manicure has been _____ on Sunday at 3:00 pm.
   A. put   B. taken   C. scheduled   D. forgotten
_____(9) Do you have any special _____ for your manicure?
   A. favor   B. outlook   C. requirements   D. blueprints
_____(10) The customer just wants a _____ manicure.
   A. regular   B. right   C. perfect   D. ugly

3. Decide whether the statement is true(T) or false(F) based on Task 3.
   _____(1) Jennifer has an appointment for a manicure today.
   _____(2) Jennifer would like a British manicure with a hint of glitter on the tips.
   _____(3) Helen will prepare the customer's nails first by filing and shaping them.
   _____(4) Jennifer will go for a square shape today.
   _____(5) Helen will gently push back the cuticles and remove any excess skin around the nail beds.
   _____(6) Helen does not offer a relaxing hand massage.
   _____(7) Once the cuticles are done, Helen will apply a color coat to protect the natural nails.
   _____(8) Helen offers a variety of nail art options.
   _____(9) There will be no drying time before the final topcoat.
   _____(10) The whole manicure process usually takes about half an hour.

4. Translate the following terms based on Task 3.
   (1) 预约_____
   (2) 法式美甲_____
   (3) 手部保湿按摩_____
   (4) 涂基础甲油_____
   (5) 美甲艺术_____
   (6) 角质层_____
   (7) 不错的选择_____
   (8) 听起来很好_____
   (9) 提供最好的服务_____
   (10) 指甲油_____

5. Fill in the blanks based on Task 4.
   (1) The manicure industry has experienced significant growth over the past _____.
   (2) One of the primary _____ contributing to the promising future of the manicure industry is the growing demand for professional manicure services.
   (3) Special occasions often _____ individuals to seek nail enhancements.
   (4) The manicure industry has evolved significantly from basic _____ and

pedicures.

(5) The diversification has _____ a larger customer base.

(6) Another factor contributing to the rapid growth of the manicure industry is the influence of social _____ platforms.

(7) The manicure industry has not been left _____ by technological advancements.

(8) LED and UV nail lamps are _____ for faster drying.

(9) The growth of the manicure industry has also created opportunities for aspiring _____.

(10) Individuals with excellent manicure skills and business _____ can establish successful ventures in this industry.

6. Match each picture with a proper expression.

(1) nail polish _____   (2) nail polish remover _____

(3) UV lamp _____   (4) emery board _____

(5) nail tips _____   (6) nail form _____

(7) nail clippers and nail scissors _____

图 6-12(选项 A)

图 6-13(选项 B)

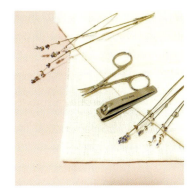

图 6-14(选项 C)

图 6-15(选项 D)

图 6-16(选项 E)

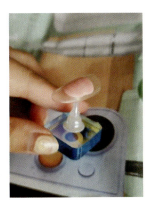

图 6-17(选项 F)

图 6-18(选项 G)

课程思政 Curriculum Ideology and Politics

Xi Jinping's Quotations 习近平语录

大力弘扬劳模精神、劳动精神、工匠精神。"不惰者,众善之师也。"在长期实践中,我们培育形成了爱岗敬业、争创一流、艰苦奋斗、勇于创新、淡泊名利、甘于奉献的劳模精神,崇尚劳动、热爱劳动、辛勤劳动、诚实劳动的劳动精神,执着专注、精益求精、一丝不苟、追求卓越的工匠精神。劳模精神、劳动精神、工匠精神是以爱国主义为核心的民族精神和以改革创新为核心的时代精神的生动体现,是鼓舞全党全国各族人民风雨无阻、勇敢前进的强大精神动力。

——选自在全国劳动模范和先进工作者表彰大会上的讲话

2020 年 11 月 24 日

We should promote the spirit of model workers, of labor, and of workmanship. There is an old Chinese saying:"All virtue comes from the absence of indolence."Over many years, we have fostered the model worker spirit of dedication to one's profession, pursuit of excellence, hard work, courageous innovation, indifference to fame and wealth, and readiness to make sacrifices; we have fostered the spirit of labor, which is about working with pride, enthusiasm, diligence, and honesty; and we have fostered the spirit of workmanship, which is defined by the relentless pursuit of perfection in a dedicated and meticulous fashion. Each of these vividly reflects our national spirit, which is centered on patriotism, and the spirit of our times, which is centered on reform and innovation, and they are a great source of strength that inspires the whole Party and all Chinese people to forge ahead through all difficulties.

——Selected from a speech at the gathering to honor model workers and exemplary individuals

November 24, 2020

Key Words and Expressions

the spirit of model workers　劳模精神

the spirit of labor　劳动精神

the spirit of workmanship　工匠精神

dedication to one's profession　爱岗敬业

pursuit of excellence　争创一流

hard work　艰苦奋斗

courageous innovation　勇于创新

indifference to fame and wealth　淡泊名利

readiness to make sacrifices　甘于奉献

working with pride, enthusiasm, diligence, and honesty　崇尚劳动、热爱劳动、辛勤劳动、诚实劳动

relentless pursuit of perfection in a dedicated and meticulous fashion　执着专注、精益求精、一丝不苟、追求卓越

forge ahead through all difficulties　风雨无阻、勇敢前进

（何丽琴　魏丹丹）

Unit 7 Cosmetology Laws and Regulations
第七单元 美容行业法律法规

扫码看 PPT

图 7-1

 Learning Objectives ┃ 学习目标

1. Understand the words and expressions in the *Safety and Technical Standards for Cosmetics*.
2. Master the words and expressions in the *Regulations on Supervision and Administration of Cosmetics*.
3. Understand the knowledge of *Measures for the Administration of Medical Cosmetology Services*.
4. Know how to write a request for leave.

Part Ⅰ Listening ┃ 听

【Instruction】

Listening is a basic skill for cosmetology application English. In this part, you

will hear a short passage. It will be read twice. For extensive listening, you should try to understand the outline of the passage. For intensive listening, the key words and expressions are important.

【Objectives】

1. First listening: Try to get the main idea of the passage.
2. Second listening: Try to get the detailed information.

Task 1 Safety and Technical Standards for Cosmetics 《化妆品安全技术规范》

【Description】

This passage is about *Safety and Technical Standards for Cosmetics* in China. When you listen for the first time, please get the main idea of the passage. After the second listening, try to choose a term in the **Word Bank** for each blank.

Word Bank

A. China Food and Drug Administration(CFDA)
   国家食品药品监督管理总局
B. *Catalogue of Prohibited Cosmetic Raw Materials*
   化妆品禁用原料目录
C. *Catalogue of Prohibited Plant (Animal) Raw Materials for Cosmetics*
   化妆品禁用植(动)物原料目录
D. cosmetic product safety report(CPSR)
   化妆品安全报告
F. Food and Drug Administration(FDA)
   美国食品药品监督管理局

In China, in order to meet the actual needs of cosmetics regulation, to combine with industry development and scientific awareness, the 1._____ has approved the issuance of the *Safety and Technical Standards for Cosmetics* (2015 version), which has come into effect on December 1, 2016.

扫码听音频1

This version of the standard provides definitions for the terms and phrases involved, clarifying the relevant concepts and their connotations. It

图 7-2　　　　　　　　　　　图 7-3

refines the general requirements for cosmetic safety technology, and revises the list of prohibited or restricted ingredients and approved ingredients for cosmetics. It revises the physical and chemical testing methods in the cosmetics inspection and evaluation methods, and standardizes the text and format of microbiological and toxicological testing methods. It revises the testing methods for evaluating human safety and efficacy. On the basis of a comparative analysis of the cosmetics-related regulations and standards of major countries and regions in the world (including the EU, the United States, Japan, South Korea, Canada, etc.), the cosmetics' safety guarantee is further improved and the adaptability and operability have been improved. It plays an important role in promoting scientific regulation of cosmetics in China, promoting the healthy development of the cosmetics industry, and enhancing the authority and international influence of China's cosmetics technical standards.

　　In 2021, the National Drug Administration released the 2._____ and the 3._____.

图 7-4

In Europe, cosmetic products regulation EC No.1223/2009 requires a detailed safety assessment—the 4. _____ before products can be marketed within the EU. Once a product is launched on the market, safety monitoring continues. Companies engage in ongoing and active monitoring of consumer experience to confirm product safety. Professionals who are specially trained in many different disciplines are involved in the design, development, and manufacture of cosmetics, such as toxicologists, microbiologists, analytical chemists, formulators, quality assurance professionals, regulatory specialists, etc.

图 7-5

In the United States, the 5. _____ monitors the safety of cosmetics in several ways. Under the United States law, cosmetic products and their ingredients do not need FDA approval before they flow into the market. Companies and individuals who market cosmetics have a legal responsibility to ensure the safety of their products. FDA periodically buys cosmetics and analyzes them. FDA scientists keep up with the latest research and conduct their own research as well.

扫码看答案 1

扫码看翻译 1

Part Ⅱ　Speaking ‖ 说

【Instruction】

Speaking is a core skill in communication. In this part, you will study a conversation about the *Regulations on Supervision and Administration of Cosmetics*.

【Objectives】

1. Master the key words and expressions.
2. Master the underlined sentences about cosmetic regulation.

Task 2　Understanding the *Regulations on Supervision and Administration of Cosmetics*
了解《化妆品监督管理条例》

【Description】

Before their internship, students Anna, Lucy and Alice are learning about the *Regulations on Supervision and Administration of Cosmetics* from their teacher, Ms. Zhang.

Think and discuss:

1. Which department is responsible for regulating cosmetics?
2. What are the provisions of the Regulation on the labeling of cosmetics?

图 7-6

图 7-7

Anna: Ms. Zhang, in what background was the *Regulations on Supervision and Administration of Cosmetics* (hereinafter referred to as the Regulation) promulgated?

Ms. Zhang: The Party Central Committee and the State Council attach great importance to product quality supervision. The Regulation is formulated to regulate cosmetics production and business activities strengthen cosmetics supervision and management, ensure the quality and safety of cosmetics, protect consumer health, and promote the healthy development of the cosmetics industry.

扫码听音频2

Anna: Exactly. Cosmetics are consumer goods that meet people's demand for beauty, thus directly affect the human body, and their quality is related to people's health.

Lucy: I learned that the Regulation consists of 80 articles in 6 chapters, which regulates from four aspects on cosmetics production and business activities, together with their supervision and management. It is effective from January 1, 2021.

扫码看翻译2

Ms. Zhang: You're right.

图 7-8

Alice: Do cosmetics mentioned in the Regulation refer to those we use every day?

Ms. Zhang: Cosmetics in the Regulation are divided into special cosmetics and ordinary cosmetics. For special cosmetics, our country implements registration management; for ordinary cosmetics, record-filing management.

Anna: Which department is responsible for regulating cosmetics?

Ms. Zhang: The drug supervision and administration department of the State Council is responsible for the supervision and administration of cosmetics nationwide. Cosmetics registrants and filling persons are responsible for the quality, safety and efficacy claims of cosmetics.

Lucy: We have learned about cosmetics labels, such as product name, ingredients, expiration date, and manufacturer. What are the provisions of the Regulation on the labeling of cosmetics?

Ms. Zhang: The Regulation stipulates that cosmetics labels should be marked with the following contents:

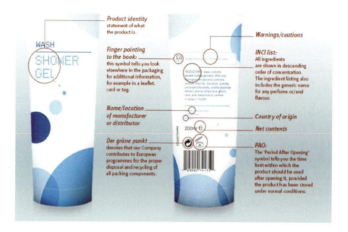

图 7-9

1. Product name and registration number of special cosmetics.

2. Name and address of the registrant, recordation entity, and the entrusted manufacturing enterprise.

3. Cosmetics production license number.

4. Standard number of the product execution.

5. Full ingredients.

6. Net content.

7. Shelf life, usage instructions and necessary safety warnings.

8. Other contents shall be marked according to laws, administrative regulations and mandatory national standards.

<u>You can browse all the details on the website of National Medical Products Administration</u> https://www.nmpa.gov.cn/.

图 7-10

Alice: Thanks, Ms. Zhang. Could you tell us something about supervision and administration regulations of cosmetics abroad?

Ms. Zhang: Sure. In the United States, the two most important laws pertaining to cosmetics marketed are the *Federal Food, Drug, and Cosmetic Act* (*FD&C Act*) and the *Fair Packaging and Labeling Act* (*FPLA*). FDA (Authority over Cosmetics) regulates cosmetics under the authority of these laws. For the EU, cosmetic products regulation EC No. 1223/2009 is the main regulatory framework for cosmetic products.

Lucy: I see. We really learnt a lot today!

Lucy, Anna, Alice: Thank you, Ms. Zhang!

Ms. Zhang: You're welcome.

Key Words and Expressions

regulation [ˌreɡjuˈleɪʃn]   n. 规章制度, 规则
provision [prəˈvɪʒn]   n. 条款, 规定
promulgate [ˈprɒmlɡeɪt]   v. 发布, 颁布（新法律）
supervision [ˌsuːpəˈvɪʒn]   n. 监督, 管理
implement [ˈɪmplɪmənt]   v. 执行, 贯彻
registration [ˌredʒɪˈstreɪʃn]   n. 登记, 注册
registrant [ˈredʒɪstrənt]   n. 注册人
be responsible for   对……负责
record-filing management   备案管理
recordation entity   备案人
consist of   由……组成
Party Central Committee   党中央
State Council   国务院

Part Ⅲ   Reading ‖ 读

【Instruction】

For a beauty practitioner, reading especially extensive reading is a necessary skill. In this part, you will study a text related to the Measures for the Administration of *Medical Cosmetology Services*.

【Objectives】

1. Understand each sub-title.
2. Try to repeat the main idea of each sub-title.

Task 3 *Measures for the Administration of Medical Cosmetology Services*
《医疗美容服务管理办法》

【Description】

Medical cosmetology has entered a period of rapid development due to the development of the Internet and the upgrading of consumption concepts. The Ministry of Health had issued *Measures for the Administration of Medical Cosmetology Services* in 2002.

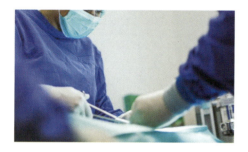

图 7-11   图 7-12

Legislation and Enforcement

Measures for the Administration of Medical Cosmetology Services is formulated to standardize medical cosmetology services, promote the healthy development of the medical cosmetology industry, and safeguard the rights and interests of medical patients. It is based on the *Law on Licensed Doctors of the People's Republic of China*, *Regulations on the Management of Medical Institutions* and *Nurse Management Measures*. It was issued by the Ministry of Health on January 22, 2002, and effective from May 1, 2002. It has been revised twice in 2009 and 2016.

扫码听
音频 3

扫码看
翻译 3

Term Definition

The term "medical cosmetology" here refers to the repair and reshaping of a person's appearance and various parts of the human body using surgery, drugs, medical equipment, and other traumatic or invasive medical technology methods.

The term "cosmetic medical institutions" here refers to medical institutions that primarily engage in the medical beauty diagnosis and treatment business.

The term "attending physician" here refers to a licensed physician who meets the prescribed conditions and is responsible for implementing medical cosmetology projects.

Graded Management

The medical cosmetic department is a Level-1 diagnostic and treatment subject, while the departments of the cosmetic surgery, cosmetic dentistry, cosmetic dermatology, and cosmetic traditional Chinese medicine are Level-2 subjects. According to the technical difficulty and potential medical risks of medical cosmetology projects, graded admission management will be implemented for medical cosmetology projects. The Ministry of Health(including the National Administration of Traditional Chinese Medicine) is responsible for the management of medical cosmetology services nationwide.

Attending Physician

The attending physician responsible for implementing medical beauty projects must meet the following requirements:

1. Having the qualification of a licensed physician and registering with the licensed physician registration authority.

2. Having relevant clinical work experience.

3. Having received professional training or further education in medical cosmetology and qualified, or having been engaged in clinical work in medical cosmetology for at least one year.

4. Other requirements stipulated by the health administrative department of the provincial people's government.

Medical cosmetology services are implemented under the responsibility of

图 7-13

the attending physician, and medical cosmetology projects must be carried out by or under the guidance of the attending physician.

Before implementing treatment, the attending physician must inform the individual or his/her relatives in written form of the indications, contraindications, medical risks and precautions for treatment, and obtain signed consent from the individual or his/her guardians.

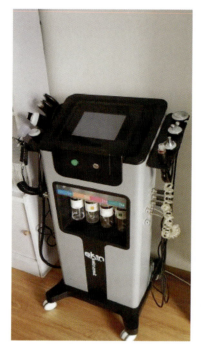

图 7-14

Privacy Protection

Practitioners of cosmetic medical institutions and medical cosmetic departments shall respect the privacy of the individual, and shall not disclose the medical conditions and medical records to a third party without the consent of the individual or his/her guardians.

Key Words and Expressions

legislation[ˌledʒɪsˈleɪʃn]　n. 立法,制定法律

enforcement[ɪnˈfɔːsmənt]　n. 执行,实施

indication[ˌɪndɪˈkeɪʃn]　n. 适应证

contraindication[ˌkɒntrəˌɪndɪˈkeɪʃn]　n. 禁忌证

precaution[prɪˈkɔːʃn]　n. 注意事项,预防措施

guardian[ˈɡɑːdɪən]   n. 监护人
qualification[ˌkwɒlɪfɪˈkeɪʃn]   n. 资格,学历
device[dɪˈvaɪs]   n. 设备,装置
Ministry of Health   卫生部
National Administration of Traditional Chinese Medicine   国家中医药管理局
medical risk   医疗风险
graded management   分级管理

Part Ⅳ Practical Writing ‖ 实用写作

【Instruction】

In the working scenario, a beauty practitioner will come across practical writing on some particular occasions. In this part, you will study a main form of beauty practical writing—request for leave.

【Objective】

Know how to write a request for leave.

Task 4 Request for Leave
请假条

【Description】

A request for leave is a written document requesting permission from a superior, a leader, a teacher, etc., for not being able to participate in a certain job, an activity or an event. It can be divided into notes for sick leave and leave for absence.

Structure：

A request for leave usually consists of three parts：

1. the title(such as Request for Leave)
2. the body(details like category, reason, leave time, etc.)
3. the signature(both the applicant's and the leader's)

图 7-15

Form：

Request for Leave

Name		Department		Number	
Category	☐Sickness　☐Annual Leave　☐Compassionate Leave　☐Others				
Reasons	 Applicant's Signature：_____				
Leave time	From _____（D）_____（M）_____（Y）to _____（D）_____（M）_____（Y）				
Reviewed and Approved by	Foreman		Signature		
	HR Manager		Signature		

Notes：

1. The reasons for requesting should be specific and clear instead of being vague.

2. The leave time must be accurate for the approver to consider and arrange.

3. The applicant should cancel the leave after the expiration date, and the leave application does not need to be withdrawn.

Example：

请假条

尊敬的张经理：

我和男友霍廷定于 2023 年 8 月 6 日举办婚礼，需要从 8 月 3 日起请假 7 天，于 8 月 10 日正常恢复上班。目前手头的工作已完成，其他工作已交付完毕。请予批准。

祝安好！

请假人：乔娜
2023 年 7 月 30 日

Request for Leave

July 30, 2023

Dear Manager Zhang,

My boyfriend Huo Ting and I will have our wedding ceremony on August 6, 2023. I need a marriage leave for one week from August 3. I am able to return to work on August 10. The work at hand has been completed, and other work has been arranged. Looking forward to your approval.

Best wishes!

Qiao Na

Summarize 项目小结

In this unit we have learnt:

1. Knowledge about standards for cosmetics, and regulation for cosmetic supervision and administration.

2. Terms and expressions about medical cosmetology services.

3. How to write a request for leave.

Test Yourself 能力检测

1. Match each English word or expression in Column A with its Chinese meaning in Column B based on Task 2.

Column A	Column B
(1) regulation	A. 执行,贯彻
(2) promulgate	B. 由……组成
(3) supervision	C. 发布,颁布(新法律)
(4) implement	D. 国家药品监督管理局
(5) registration	E. 备案人
(6) consist of	F. 国务院
(7) Party Central Committee	G. 监督,管理
(8) State Council	H. 党中央
(9) National Medical Products Administration	I. 规章制度,规则
(10) recordation entity	J. 登记,注册

2. Choose the best answer based on Task 2.

____ (1) The Party Central Committee and the State Council _____ great importance to product quality supervision.

A. get B. attach
C. through D. cancel

____(2)The Regulation _____ of 80 articles in 6 chapters.

A. because B. makes up
C. learns D. consists

____(3)Cosmetics in the Regulation are divided into _____ cosmetics and ordinary cosmetics.

A. special　　B. expensive　　C. excellent　　D. colored

____(4)Which department is responsible for regulating cosmetics?

A. the drug supervision and administration department

B. the financial department

C. the judicial department

D. the medical department

____(5)Cosmetics _____ should be marked with cosmetics production license number.

A. forms　　B. containers　　C. labels　　D. bags

____(6)Net content should be marked on cosmetics labels.

A. wrong　　B. right　　C. not mentioned　　D. uncertain

____(7)You can browse all the details on the _____ of National Medical Products Administration.

A. page　　B. website　　C. office　　D. book

____(8)In the United States, the two most important laws pertaining to cosmetics marketed are _____.

A. *FD&C Act*, *FPLA* B. *FPLA*, *FBI*
C. *FD&C Act*, *FDPC* D. *FD&C Act*, *DA*

____(9)For the EU, cosmetic products regulation EC No. 1223/2009 is the main regulatory _____ for cosmetic products.

A. teamwork　　B. outwork　　C. framework　　D. network

____(10)For students before an internship, knowing the Regulation is very helpful.

A. wrong　　B. right　　C. not mentioned　　D. uncertain

3. Decide whether the statement is true(T) or false(F) based on Task 3.

____(1)*Measures for the Administration of Medical Cosmetology Services* is issued by the Ministry of Health.

____(2)*Measures for the Administration of Medical Cosmetology Services* has been revised once.

____(3) The term "medical cosmetology" here refers to the repair and reshaping of a person's appearance and no parts of the human body.

____(4) The term "attending physician" here refers to a licensed physician who meets the prescribed conditions and is responsible for implementing medical cosmetology projects.

____(5) The medical cosmetic department is a Level-1 diagnostic and treatment subject.

____(6) The Ministry of Health is responsible for the management of medical cosmetology services nationwide.

____(7) The attending physician must have the qualification of a licensed physician and register with the licensed physician registration authority.

____(8) Medical cosmetology services are implemented under the responsibility of the manager.

____(9) Practitioners of cosmetic medical institutions shall respect the privacy of the individual.

____(10) Practitioners shall not disclose the individual's medical conditions to a third party without consent.

4. Translate the following terms based on Task 3.

(1) 分级管理_____

(2) 隐私保护_____

(3) 主诊医师_____

(4) 卫生部_____

(5) 医疗器械_____

(6) 监护人_____

(7) 医疗风险_____

(8) 美容医疗机构_____

(9) 美容外科_____

(10) 禁忌证_____

5. Writing practice based on Task 4.

说明：假设你叫王芳，因阑尾炎需手术和住院治疗一周，需要向部门经理张兰请假。请假时间：2023年7月10日至7月17日。就诊医院：河北省人民医院。请用英语写一则请假条。申请日期：2023年7月9日。

_____
_____
_____
_____
_____

课程思政　Curriculum Ideology and Politics

传统文化赏析：*Han Feizi · Having Regulations*《韩非子·有度》

国无常强，无常弱。奉法者强，则国强；奉法者弱，则国弱。……故当今之时，能去私曲就公法者，民安而国治；能去私行行公法者，则兵强而敌弱。故审得失有法度之制者，加以群臣之上，则主不可欺以诈伪；审得失有权衡之称者，以听远事，则主不可欺以天下之轻重。

图 7-16

No country is permanently strong. Nor is any country permanently weak. If the conformers to the law are strong, the country will be strong; if conformers to the law are weak, the country will be weak. ... Therefore, at present, any ruler who is able to expel private crookedness and uphold public law finds the people safe and the state in order; any ruler who is able to expunge private action and act on public law finds his army strong and his enemy weak. So find out men following the discipline of laws and regulations, and place them above the body of officials, thus the sovereign cannot be deceived by anybody with fraud and falsehood. Find out men able to weigh different situations, and put them in charge of distant affairs, thus the sovereign cannot be deceived by anybody in matters of world politics.

Key Words and Expressions

expel[ɪkˈspel]　v. 驱逐,排除

discipline[ˈdɪsəplɪn]　n. 纪律,风纪

conformer[kənˈfɔːmə]　n. 奉行者

sovereign[ˈsɒvrɪn]　n. 君主

politics[ˈpɒlətɪks]　n. 政治,局势,观念

（魏丹丹　邓叶青）

Unit 8　Communication and Service
第八单元　沟通与服务

扫码看
PPT

图 8-1

Learning Objectives ┃ 学习目标

1. Describe a process for a massage service in a beauty salon.
2. Master words and expressions for introducing products.
3. Master words and expressions for verbal and non-verbal communication skills in a beauty salon.
4. Master skills for verbal and non-verbal communication in a beauty salon.
5. Know how to write a letter of thanks.

Part Ⅰ　Listening ┃ 听

【Instruction】

Listening is a basic skill for cosmetology application English. In this part, you

will hear a short passage about the process of a back massage service. It will be read twice. For the first time, you should be able to identify the main points. For the second time, you should be able to obtain key details and important information.

【Objectives】

1. Develop listening skills to obtain the main idea of the passage.
2. Develop listening skills to obtain key details and important information of the passage.

Task 1　A Process for a Massage Service
　　　　　　按摩服务流程

【Description】

In a beauty salon, there are procedures to follow in a back massage service. The standard procedures help to guarantee the quality of service. Listen to the passage and choose a correct answer from the **Word Bank** for each blank.

图 8-2

> **Word Bank**
> A. consultation　　B. tailored treatment　　C. feedback
> D. procedures　　E. preparations

Nowadays, massage is one of the most popular services available in a beauty salon. Massage therapy helps to reduce stress and relieve pain. To provide great massage services for clients, there are some 1._____to follow. Take the process of a back massage service for a lady as an example. In the whole process for a back massage service, the procedures can be divided into three parts: pre-service procedure, actual service procedure and post-service procedure.

扫码听
音频1

Pre-Service Procedure

In the pre-service procedure, make sure all 2._____ are complete before the client comes. Firstly, clean the massage room and bed to create a hygienic and comfortable environment for a back massage. Next, prepare disinfected tools, implements and materials, such as body massage rollers, towels, gowns and massage oil. In addition, always remember to maintain a professional appearance, good personal hygiene and hands well cared. If hands are cold, do some hand exercises to warm hands and don't touch the client's back with cold hands.

Actual Service Procedure

In the actual service procedure, it is essential to provide professional services for the client. These services include meeting and greeting the client, performing a consultation, helping the client prepare for the back massage, palpation assessment and performing a back massage.

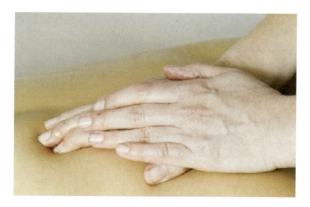

图 8-3

Meeting and Greeting

Firstly, meet and greet the lady with a smile.

Performing a Client Consultation

Then, provide a 3._____ to the lady. In the consultation, make an effective communication with the client and request her to fill out a client intake form to know her basic personal information and health history. Pay particular attention to the client's allergic history and do not use any product that would cause her allergies.

Besides, it is important to identify her needs and preference.

A Client's Preparation for Back Massage

Next, escort the client to a separate massage room. In the massage room, request the client to change into a gown and remove jewelry that can be damaged or hurt her body during the back massage.

图 8-4

A Palpation Assessment

A palpation assessment can help to identify problems that the client has. Ask the client to lie face-down on her belly on the massage bed and touch her back to perform a palpation assessment. According to the assessment, create a 4. _____ to satisfy the needs and requirements of the client.

Performing a Back Massage

After above steps, perform appropriate back manipulations, such as kneading, muscle rolling, wringing, hacking and clapping to press the client's back and relieve her back pain. When finishing this back massage, the client lies on the massage bed to have a rest.

Post-Service Procedure

In the post-service procedure, ask the client for 5. _____ on this massage service and give her some advice to care back at home, which makes her feel valued. Lastly, request payment for this massage service, schedule the next appointment with her and don't forget to say thanks to the client.

扫码看答案 1

扫码看翻译 1

Part Ⅱ　　Speaking ‖ 说

【Instruction】

Speaking is a core skill in communicating with clients, introducing programs, recommending products, etc. In this part, you will learn a conversation about introducing products.

【Objective】

Master the underlined sentences for introducing products.

Task 2　　Introducing Products
推介产品

【Description】

A client has acne on her face. The beauty adviser is helping her to diagnose the skin problem and introducing her the products to get better.

Think and discuss:

1. What are the causes of acne problems?
2. What is the best treatment for acne problems?

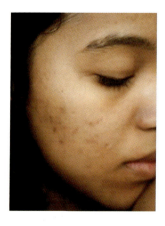
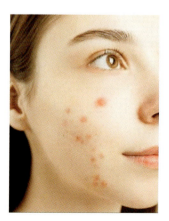

图 8-5　　　　　　　　　　　图 8-6

Lisa—a beauty adviser   Joy Smith—a client

Lisa: Welcome, Miss Smith. This way please.

Joy: Thank you.

Lisa: Do you want to have face care or body care today?

Joy: Face care.

扫码听
音频 2

Lisa: I find you have a few pimples on your cheeks and forehead. How long have they been there?

Joy: About two weeks. The pimples keep cropping up.

Lisa: You have the acne-prone skin. It's a common skin care problem. Don't worry.

扫码看
翻译 2

Joy: What causes the pimples to develop?

Lisa: There are many influences. Some pimples are caused by an imbalance of hormones in the body. Some pimples break out because of the strong sebum secretion, which can block pores, reproduce bacteria and trigger acne. Staying up late or eating spicy food can also lead to breakouts.

Joy: Oh. That's too annoying.

Lisa: Yes. It should be treated properly or it will leave acne scars on your skin. Right?

Joy: That's too bad. What should I do now?

Lisa: It's not difficult. The key is to improve skin condition and activate skin liveness. I recommend that you have the acne treatment program in our shop. Should I give you an introduction to the program?

Joy: All right.

图 8-7

Lisa: Clear with a needle before using our products. This acne treatment kit includes four pieces: mask, anti-acne serum, toner and lotion. The mask contains serum ingredients that can deeply repair the skin and kill bacteria, as well as fine pores and remove excess oil. After removing the mask, use anti-acne serum, pat on toner and lotion to consolidate the effect. What's more, it's a Chinese herbal formula with a gentle nature. The products help promote cell regeneration, speed up metabolism, eliminate breakouts and prevent scarring and marks.

Joy: How long will it take effect?

Lisa: The inflammation can be monitored after you clean up today. Your skin will feel smooth in a few days. After a week of healing, you can see obvious results.

Joy: Sounds good.

Lisa: In order to consolidate the effect, I suggest you come for a treatment once a week. Do you have the time?

Joy: I have a lot of time lately.

Lisa: That's great. The pimples will be almost cured in two months. Healthy skincare is always a significant concern for women.

Joy: How much is it?

Lisa: We are here to help you achieve the best result without having to spend much. The acne treatment program values 1980 yuan. How do you like it?

Joy: Then I will take it.

Lisa: OK. Let me pack the products for you.

图 8-8

Key Words and Expressions

pimple['pɪmpl]　n. 痤疮，粉刺

sebum['si:bəm]　n. 皮脂

secretion[sɪˈkriːʃən]　n. 分泌,分泌物
pore[pɔː]　n.（皮肤上的）毛孔,（植物的）气孔,孔隙
scar[skɑː]　n. 瘢痕,伤痕
mask[mɑːsk]　n. 面膜,面罩
serum[ˈsɪərəm]　n. 精华素,乳清,血清
toner[ˈtəʊnə]　n. 爽肤水,墨粉
herbal[ˈhɜːbl]　adj. 药草的　n. 草本植物志
regeneration[rɪˌdʒenəˈreɪʃn]　n. 再生,重生
metabolism[məˈtæbəlɪzəm]　n. 新陈代谢
inflammation[ˌɪnfləˈmeɪʃn]　n. 炎症,发炎
crop up　出现,发生
take effect　产生效果

Part Ⅲ　Reading ‖ 读

【Instruction】

Reading skills are essential in the workplace. In this part, you will read two texts about communication, and learn knowledge and skills for verbal and non-verbal communication in a beauty salon.

【Objectives】

1. Master key words, phrases and sentence structures of the two texts.
2. Master verbal communication skills for a beauty adviser.
3. Master non-verbal communication skills for a beautician.

Task 3　Verbal Communication Skills
语言沟通技巧

【Description】

Verbal communication is essential in our daily lives. It refers to the use of words to exchange information. Effective verbal communication is helpful in building positive and strong relationships at work and providing good service for clients.

图 8-9

Verbal communication plays a vital role in daily life. It is one type of communication and refers to the use of words to exchange information between two or more people to create mutual understanding. All of these actions, such as reading books, talking with families or friends, listening to music and writing letters, are related to verbal communication. Effective verbal communication could help people get news and information, acquire knowledge and skills, express point of view, exchange emotions and thoughts to develop interpersonal relationships and so on. Therefore, it is important to develop effective verbal communication skills. Especially in a workplace, effective verbal communication skills can help staff build positive relationships with bosses, colleagues and clients, which is beneficial to career advancement.

扫码听音频 3

扫码看翻译 3

If you are a beauty adviser, how to develop effective verbal communication skills at work? Supposing you will offer a consultation about back massage to a lady, how to deliver her great service through verbal communication? Firstly, remember to work professionally to satisfy your client. Your services should be professional and meet the client's needs and expectations. Always use positive and courteous words, keep your tone of voice polite and speak at a moderate pace, which will make her feel respected and comfortable. When greeting the lady, give a warm welcome verbally and use words like "Good morning, Madam". If she is a regular client, you can start a conversation with her by small talk to build a stronger relationship. For instance, a compliment on the client's hairstyle can be a good choice. After that, identify the client's preferences and needs. You should listen to her attentively and it is better

图 8-10

not to interrupt her until she finishes talking. Then, ask the client some open-ended questions to get more details about the massage service. If the client feels back pain, you can ask her what it feels like. This may help you know why she suffers from back pain and create a tailored treatment plan for her. Besides, it is necessary to repeat what the client has said before her, which helps to confirm her desires and avoid misunderstanding. If the client asks you some questions about the service, you can answer professionally by using some proper terminologies, and at the same time explain clearly by using some simple words and examples. Make sure to speak in precise terms but not vague terms. Otherwise, your client may feel confused, misunderstand what you say and be dissatisfied with your service. Last but not least, never argue with your client when some unhappy events occur. Instead, listen to her empathically and try to explain what happens tactfully. These are the keys for a beauty adviser to achieving successful communication with a client.

Verbal communication is essential for people's interaction. Without effective verbal communication, there may be conflict and misunderstanding between people. In a beauty salon, effective verbal communication could help to win clients' trust, make clients enjoy their experiences and boost clients' satisfaction. Therefore, as staff in a beauty salon, it is important to develop effective verbal communication skills and become excellent communicators.

图 8-11

Key Words and Expressions

verbal['vɜːbl] adj. 语言的,文字的
understanding[ˌʌndəˈstændɪŋ] n. 理解,了解,谅解
interpersonal[ˌɪntəˈpɜːsənl] adj. 人际的,人际关系的
consultation[ˌkɒnslˈteɪʃn] n. 咨询,商讨
expectation[ˌekspekˈteɪʃn] n. 预期,期望
moderate[ˈmɒdərət] adj. 适度的,适中的,温和的
preference[ˈprefrəns] n. 偏爱,喜爱,偏爱的事物
terminology[ˌtɜːmɪˈnɒlədʒɪ] n.(某学科的)术语,专门用语
precise[prɪˈsaɪs] adj. 精确的,准确的,确切的
dissatisfied[dɪsˈsætɪsfaɪd] adj.(对……)不满的,不满意的
tactfully[ˈtæktfəlɪ] adv. 巧妙地,言行得体地

Task 4　Non-Verbal Communication Skills
　　　　 非语言沟通技巧

【Description】

Non-verbal communication is to convey a message without words. Non-verbal communication has to do with physical appearance, body language, space and so on. For a beautician in a beauty salon, following non-verbal communication skills helps to provide better service for clients and create better work performance.

图 8-12

Good communication is the beginning of a harmonious relationship and is valuable to a business. In daily life, we use verbal communication which is related to words. However, the keys to successful communication are far more than words. We can convey our feelings or thoughts through physical appearance, body language, space and so on. These are the ways how non-verbal communication works. In fact, about 58% of messages are sent through non-verbal communication. As the saying goes, "Silence is more powerful than words." In a beauty salon, a beautician should learn some non-verbal communication skills so as to provide better service for clients and create better work performance.

扫码听音频

扫码看翻译

Here are some types of non-verbal communication.

A person's physical appearance, including appearance and clothing is a silent language and an intangible business card in communication. The elegant and neat appearance, such as light makeup and unified work uniform, not only constitutes the personal charm of a beautician, but also helps to make a good first impression on clients.

Body language, including postures, gestures, facial expressions, eye contact, etc., plays an important part in communication. The feelings and emotions conveyed by body language are richer and more attractive and persuasive. Good standing, sitting, walking and squatting postures are essential, which demonstrate the spirit and etiquette of a beautician. Facial expression can present yourself well visually. A

图 8-13

smiling face is the most beautiful. With a smile and a vivid expression on the face, a beautician definitely gives the client a feeling of familiarity that feels at home. Instead, a stiff and rigid expression hardly makes the client feel the sincerity of service. A beautician also needs to control expressions such as dislike, disgust, hostility, etc., which are prone to misunderstanding. The eye contact may be a signal of hope for communication, showing interest, respect and willingness to listen. A good beautician should always keep eye contact with the client because it is an excellent response. Therefore, the client will feel that she is valued and respected. On the other hand, too long a gaze can make people uncomfortable.

Space means the body distance you stay from the client. It indicates the closeness between you and the client. When a new client enters the shop, a beautician stands up with a head nodding and a smile as a gesture of welcome to the client. It's impolite to stand too close to her. While for a regular client, you can even hold her hand or arm, or hug her shoulder, showing her the way to the beauty salon room.

What's more, in the process of communication with the client, a beautician should pay attention to the rate of speech, the tone of voice, laughing or silence. That's the paralanguage, which means how you say it rather than what is said.

Non-verbal communication, together with the verbal communication transfers information a lot. Apparently, it's essential to be aware of the impact of non-verbal communication and follow the proper non-verbal communication skills. A beautician should consciously and further use them in the work.

图 8-14

Key Words and Expressions

non-verbal[ˌnɒnˈvɜːbl] adj. 非语言的
beautician[bjuːˈtɪʃn] n. 美容师
intangible[ɪnˈtændʒəbl] adj. 无形的
constitute[ˈkɒnstɪtjuːt] v. 组成，构成
posture[ˈpɒstʃə(r)] n.（坐，立的）姿势，态度，立场
gesture[ˈdʒestʃə(r)] n. 手势，示意动作
squat[skwɒt] v. 蹲
etiquette[ˈetɪket] n. 礼节，礼仪，规矩
facial[ˈfeɪʃl] adj. 面部的
familiarity[fəˌmɪliˈærəti] n. 亲近，友好随和
rigid[ˈrɪdʒɪd] adj. 僵硬的，死板的，固执的
beauty salon 美容院

Part Ⅳ Practical Writing ‖ 实用写作

【Instruction】

In the working scenario, a beauty practitioner will come across practical writing on some particular occasions. In this part, you will study a main form of beauty practical writing—letter of thanks.

【Objective】

Know how to write a letter of thanks.

Task 5　Letter of Thanks
感谢信

【Description】

A letter of thanks will be sent to show that you are grateful to someone for what he or she has done, like the support, help or warm hospitality.

Structure:

A letter of thanks usually consists of three parts:

1. the title

2. the body

(1) expressing thanks

(2) explaining reasons

(3) expressing thanks again and expressing wishes to return clients

3. the signature

Example:

A Letter of Thanks

Dear Mary,

I am writing the letter for the purpose of extending my sincere gratitude to you.

I hope you know how much I appreciate your continuous care, support, trust and hospitality for my work at the beauty salon during this year. I am pleased that you are satisfied with my service and trust in our beauty products. That's the source and motivation for my growth. I would also like to thank you for your advice and feedback on my work, which I find very informative and useful.

Again, please accept my heartfelt gratitude. I hope that I will have the opportunity to return your kindness. And I'm eagerly expecting to provide you with the sincerest and highest quality service in the coming new year. Wish you health and happiness.

Yours truly,

Lisa

Amelie Beauty Salon

Summarize 项目小结

In this unit we have learnt:

1. Knowledge about the process of a massage service in a beauty salon.

2. How to introduce beauty products.

3. Knowledge and skills for verbal and non-verbal communication.

4. How to write a letter of thanks.

Test Yourself 能力检测

1. Match each English word or expression in Column A with its Chinese meaning in Column B based on Task 1.

Column A	Column B
(1) relieve	A. （正式或礼貌地）请
(2) procedure	B. 安排
(3) kneading	C. 揉捏
(4) disinfected	D. 按摩手法
(5) hygiene	E. 消毒的
(6) request	F. 触诊评估
(7) client intake form	G. 步骤
(8) preference	H. 客户登记表
(9) massage manipulation	I. 卫生
(10) palpation assessment	J. 缓解
(11) allergy	K. 偏好
(12) schedule	L. 过敏

扫码看
答案 2

2. Listen to the passage of Task 1 and put the following statements in the correct order.

A. In the actual service procedure, it is essential to provide professional services for the client.

B. Perform an effective consultation, and identify needs, preferences and health history of this client.

C. Before a back massage, make sure all preparations are complete before the client comes.

D. Perform a palpation assessment to identify problems that the client has and create a tailored treatment for her.

E. Request payment for this service, schedule the next appointment with the client and don't forget to say thanks to her.

F. After the back massage, ask for feedback on this service from the client and give her some advice to care back at home.

G. Create a hygienic and comfortable environment, and maintain a professional appearance, good personal hygiene and hands well cared.

Answer: _____

3. Decide whether the statement is true(T) or false(F) based on Task 2.

____(1) Acne may be caused by hormone imbalance in the body.

____(2) Acne occurs for a variety of reasons.

____(3) Staying up late will not cause acne.

____(4) If untreated, pimples don't leave scars.

____(5) Needle-clearing is required first to remove the acne.

____(6) There are three pieces contained in the acne treatment kit.

____(7) After using the acne treatment products, it can speed up metabolism and activate the skin's liveness.

____(8) Healthy skincare is always an important concern for women.

4. Choose the best answer based on the passages of Task 3 and Task 4.

____(1) Verbal communication refers to the use of _____ to exchange information.

  A. words   B. gestures   C. sound   D. tools

____(2) Effective verbal communication skills help staff achieve _____.

  A. consensus   B. a goal

  C. independence   D. career advancement

____(3) To deliver great client service, a beauty adviser should meet a client's _____.

  A. respect and trust   B. needs and expectations

  C. needs and trust   D. respect and expectations

____(4) A beauty adviser can start a conservation with a client by _____ to build a stronger relationship.

  A. formal discussions   B. a try story

  C. small talk   D. open-ended questions

____(5) A beauty adviser should answer a client's questions in _____ terms.

  A. precise   B. possible   C. vague   D. polite

____(6) Besides verbal communication, _____ plays an important part for people's interaction.

A. a short silence B. a serious tone

C. non-verbal communication D. a loud voice

____(7) Non-verbal communication skills help a beautician to _____.

A. provide better service for clients B. earn more money

C. become a leader D. achieve success

____(8) The _____ makes a good impression on clients.

A. thoughts and emotion B. requirement and desire

C. theory and practice D. elegant and neat appearance

____(9) A smiling face makes clients feel _____.

A. unhappy and disappointed B. comfortable and relaxed

C. surprised and confused D. embarrassed and uneasy

____(10) A stiff and rigid expression cause _____ communication.

A. negative B. powerful C. traditional D. perfect

5. Writing practice based on Task 5.

说明：假设你是爱美丽美容院的工作人员，值此十周年庆典之际，请用英语写一封感谢信，感谢顾客对美容院工作的关心、支持和信任。

_____
_____
_____
_____
_____

课程思政 Curriculum Ideology and Politics

榜样的力量：巴渝工匠李真芹（简介）

李真芹，重庆城市管理职业学院教师，世界技能大赛美容项目国家队教练。2019年俄罗斯喀山第45届世界技能大赛美容项目银牌获得者，2019年澳大利亚全球技能挑战赛美容项目金牌获得者；获全国技术能手、全国青年岗位能手、巴渝特级技师、重庆市巾帼建功标兵、巴渝最美工匠等荣誉称号。她致力于将世界技能大赛美容项目的标准和技术推广到职业教育中，落实到世界技能大赛训练中，为我国培养更多优秀的美容技术人才。

Power of a Role Model: Bayu Craftsman Li Zhenqin

Spirit of craftsmanship can be defined as a pursuit of excellence, dedication to work and innovation. Li Zhenqin, a cosmetology teacher and coach for the WorldSkills Competition from Chongqing City Management

College, has interpreted the spirit of craftsmanship through her beliefs, actions and achievements.

When Li Zhenqin was a student at Chongqing University of Science and Technology, she won first prize in the beauty event at the China Skills Competition in 2018, and was successfully selected to the national team of beauty event for the 45th WorldSkills Competition. In the national team, Li Zhenqin realized that finely honed technical skills were the key to win the competition. Therefore, she focused on excellence skills, delved deep into theories about cosmetology and honed her skills for beauty therapy day and night. Her hard work and persistence paid off, and in August 2019, she won the silver medal in the beauty therapy contest at the 45th WorldSkills Competition in Kazan, Russia. Li Zhenqin's pursuit of vocational excellence takes her to the world platform on which she has showcased a Chinese technician's superb skills and spirit of craftsmanship to the world. After graduation, Li Zhenqin joined Chongqing City Management College and became a cosmetology teacher and coach for the WorldSkills Competition. As a teacher and coach, she still adheres to the spirit of craftsmanship and pursues excellence in teaching. She integrates WorldSkills Competition occupational standards for beauty therapy into teaching, unreservedly passes on her experience and skills to students, and cultivates excellent beauty technicians for China.

Li Zhenqin inherits and carries forward the spirit of craftsmanship. She has won many honorary titles, such as National Technical Expert, National Youth Post Expert, Bayu Craftsman and Chongqing Women Pacesetters. All of these can reflect her spirit as a superb craftsman. Li Zhenqin has become a role model for young people, inspiring them to pursue excellence skills and serve our motherland.

扫码看
翻译 5

——Adapted from the *Chongqing Daily* report, *Li Zhenqin: Skills to Decorate Life and Spirit of Craftsmanship to Empower Beauty*

December 15, 2022

Key Words and Expressions

hone [həʊn]　v. 磨炼，训练（尤指技艺）

vocational [vəʊˈkeɪʃənl] adj. 职业的
WorldSkills Competition 世界技能大赛
beauty therapy 美容（护理）
occupational standards 职业标准

（周　彧　姚　艳）

Appendix A　Vocabulary for Self-Test
附录A　自助记忆词汇表

使用方法:将此页从中间向后折叠,对照左侧英文,写出词性和词义,或对照右侧中文,写出英文单词。

Unit 1

1. major[ˈmeɪdʒə(r)] _____ n. 专业　v. 主修　adj. 主要的
2. freshman[ˈfreʃmən] _____ n.(中学或大学的)一年级新生
3. cosmetology[ˌkɒzməˈtɒlədʒɪ] _____ n. 整容术,美容术,美容学
4. cosmetic[kɒzˈmetɪk] _____ n. 化妆品　adj. 美容的
5. technology[tekˈnɒlədʒɪ] _____ n. 技术,科技
6. department[dɪˈpɑːtmənt] _____ n. 系,部门,科室
7. client[ˈklaɪənt] _____ n. 顾客,客户
8. major in _____ 以……为专业
9. medical cosmetic technology _____ 医学美容技术
10. beauty education and management _____ 美容教育与管理
11. traditional Chinese medicine healthcare _____ 传统中医养生
12. make it _____ 及时到达,(非正式)成功
13. angel[ˈeɪndʒl] _____ n. 天使,天使般的人
14. salon[ˈsælɒn] _____ n. 客厅,沙龙
15. decorate[ˈdekəreɪt] _____ v. 装饰,布置,装修
16. relaxation[ˌriːlækˈseɪʃn] _____ n. 放松,消遣,松弛
17. elegant[ˈelɪɡənt] _____ adj. 优雅的,雅致的
18. comfortable[ˈkʌmftəbl] _____ adj. 令人舒适的,安逸的
19. environment[ɪnˈvaɪrənmənt] _____ n. 环境,外界,周围
20. charge[tʃɑːdʒ] _____ v. 要价　n. 责任,费用
21. double[ˈdʌbl] _____ adj. 双重的,成双的
22. beauty salon/shop _____ 美容院
23. reception room _____ 接待室,接待区

Appendix A   Vocabulary for Self-Test │ 附录 A   自助记忆词汇表

24. dressing table _____ 梳妆台
25. batching room _____ 配料间
26. show sb. around _____ 带（某人）参观
27. status['steɪtəs] _____ n.（进展的）状况,地位,身份
28. constant['kɒnstənt] _____ adj. 不断的,连续发生的
29. innovate['ɪnəveɪt] _____ v. 革新,创新
30. functional['fʌŋkʃənl] _____ adj. 实用的,功能的
31. ingredient[ɪn'griːdɪənt] _____ n.（食品的）成分,原料
32. pay attention to _____ 对（某人/某事）注意
33. in short _____ 总之,简言之

Unit 2

1. receptionist[rɪ'sepʃnɪst] _____ n. 接待员
2. leaflet['liːflət] _____ n. 宣传单
3. promote[prə'məʊt] _____ v. 促进,推动
4. moisture['mɔɪstʃə(r)] _____ n. 滋润
5. discount['dɪskaʊnt] _____ n. 折扣
6. pay back _____ 回馈
7. regular client _____ 老顾客,常客
8. facial treatment _____ 面部护理
9. promotional campaigns _____ 促销活动
10. reservation[ˌrezə'veɪʃn] _____ n. 预订
11. arrange[ə'reɪndʒ] _____ v. 安排
12. beautician[bjuː'tɪʃn] _____ n. 美容师
13. provincial[prə'vɪnʃəl] _____ adj. 省级的
14. acupressure['ækjupreʃə(r)] _____ n. 指压
15. radiant['reɪdɪənt] _____ adj. 容光焕发的
16. blemish['blemɪʃ] _____ n. 斑点,瑕疵 v. 破坏……的完美
17. organ['ɔːgən] _____ n. 器官
18. function['fʌŋkʃn] _____ n. 功能
19. sunscreen['sʌnskriːn] _____ n. 防晒霜(油)
20. melanin['melənɪn] _____ n. 黑色素
21. tan[tæn] _____ n. 棕褐色肤色 v. 晒黑
22. ward[wɔːd] _____ v. 躲开,避开,防止

23. shrink [ʃrɪŋk] v.收缩
24. genetics [dʒɪ'netɪks] n.遗传学,遗传特征
25. acne ['æknɪ] n.痤疮,粉刺
26. diet ['daɪət] n.日常饮食
27. make sense 合乎情理
28. ward off 躲开,避开,防止

Unit 3

1. analysis [ə'næləsɪs] n.分析,解析
2. apparatus [ˌæpə'reɪtəs] n.器官,装置,机构,组织,仪器
3. spicy ['spaɪsɪ] adj.辣的
4. shrimp [ʃrɪmp] n.虾
5. cautious ['kɔːʃəs] adj.小心的,谨慎的,慎重的
6. cheek [tʃiːk] n.面颊
7. moisturize ['mɔɪstʃəraɪz] v.给……增加水分,使……湿润
8. skin analysis apparatus 皮肤分析仪
9. be prone to 倾向于……
10. necklace ['nekləs] n.项链
11. earring ['ɪərɪŋ] n.耳环
12. gown [gaun] n.长袍
13. sprayer ['spreɪə(r)] n.喷雾机
14. exfoliation [eksˌfəʊlɪ'eɪʃn] n.去角质
15. massage ['mæsɑːʒ] n.按摩,推拿 v.按摩,推拿
16. faint [feɪnt] adj.微弱的,模糊的,暗淡的
17. residue ['rezɪdjuː] n.残渣,剩余物
18. refreshed [rɪ'freʃt] adj 精力充沛的,恢复活力的
19. scrubbing cream 磨砂膏
20. essential oil 精油
21. stubborn ['stʌbən] adj.有决心的,顽强的,坚持不懈的
22. tighten ['taɪtn] v.拉紧,拽紧,加强,强化
23. adjust [ə'dʒʌst] v.调整,调好,整理,评定,适应
24. beautification [ˌbjuːtɪfɪ'keɪʃn] n.美化
25. complexion [kəm'plekʃn] n.肤色,面色,性质,气质
26. plug [plʌg] v.填塞,插入

27. penetrate[ˈpenɪtreɪt] _____ v. 透入,渗入,透过
28. photon skin rejuvenation device _____ 光子嫩肤仪
29. stubborn skin problems _____ 顽固的皮肤问题
30. user manual _____ 用户手册

Unit 4

1. compliment[ˈkɒmplɪmənt] _____ n. 赞扬,称赞 v. 赞美,恭维
2. uneasy[ʌnˈiːzi] _____ adj. 心神不安的,不舒服的
3. stiff[stɪf] _____ adj. 僵硬的
4. vessel[ˈvesl] _____ n. 血管
5. tension[ˈtenʃn] _____ n. 紧张,不安 v. 使紧张,使不安
6. available[əˈveɪləbl] _____ adj. 有空的,可获得的
7. circulation[ˌsɜːkjuˈleɪʃn] _____ n. 循环
8. stiff neck _____ 落枕
9. take...into consideration _____ 考虑
10. stagnation[stæɡˈneɪʃn] _____ n. 停滞
11. intolerable[ɪnˈtɒlərəbl] _____ adj. 无法忍受的
12. diagnosis[ˌdaɪəɡˈnəʊsɪs] _____ n. 诊断,判断
13. invasion[ɪnˈveɪʒn] _____ n. 入侵,侵略
14. blockage[ˈblɒkɪdʒ] _____ n. 堵塞
15. node[nəʊd] _____ n. 节,瘤,结节
16. rejuvenate[rɪˈdʒuːvəneɪt] _____ v. 使……年轻,使……恢复精神
17. reflection[rɪˈflekʃn] _____ n. 反射,反映
18. reproduction[ˌriːprəˈdʌkʃn] _____ n. 生殖
19. clot[klɒt] _____ n. 凝块,堵塞物
20. dizzy[ˈdɪzi] _____ adj. 头昏眼花的,使人头晕的
21. insomnia[ɪnˈsɒmniə] _____ n. 失眠
22. constipation[ˌkɒnstɪˈpeɪʃn] _____ n. 便秘
23. air-conditioning room _____ 空调房
24. oriental[ˌɔːriˈentl] _____ adj. 东方的,东方人的
25. dynamics[daɪˈnæmɪks] _____ n. 动力学,动态原理
26. five elements _____ 五行
27. associate with _____ 与……相联系
28. *Huangdi Neijing* (*Inner Canon of Huangdi*) _____ 《黄帝内经》

29. be fundamental to _____ 对……很重要

Unit 5

1. embellish[ɪmˈbelɪʃ] _____ v. 美化,装饰,修饰
2. enhance[ɪnˈhɑːns] _____ v. 提高,增加,加强
3. foundation[faʊnˈdeɪʃn] _____ n. 粉底
4. defect[ˈdiːfekt] _____ n. 瑕疵,毛病
5. modify[ˈmɒdɪfaɪ] _____ v. 修饰,修改
6. triangle[ˈtraɪæŋgl] _____ n. 三角形
7. gloomy[ˈgluːmɪ] _____ adj. 暗淡的,阴暗的
8. mascara[mæˈskɑːrə] _____ n. 睫毛膏
9. lipstick[ˈlɪpstɪk] _____ n. 口红
10. crucial[ˈkruːʃl] _____ adj. 关键的,决定性的
11. permanently[ˈpɜːmənəntlɪ] _____ adv. 永久地
12. magical[ˈmædʒɪkl] _____ adj. 神奇的,奇妙的
13. eye shadow _____ 眼影
14. blush compact _____ 腮红
15. wedding[ˈwedɪŋ] _____ n. 婚礼,结婚庆典
16. bride[braɪd] _____ n. 新娘
17. focus[ˈfəʊkəs] _____ n. 焦点,中心 v. 聚焦,调整
18. spray[spreɪ] _____ v. 喷,喷射 n. 喷雾,喷雾器
19. smear[smɪə] _____ v. 涂抹,敷
20. neckline[ˈneklaɪn] _____ n. 领口
21. tissue[ˈtɪʃuː] _____ n. 纸巾
22. sewing[ˈsəʊɪŋ] _____ n. 缝纫,缝制物
23. kit[kɪt] _____ n. 成套工具,工具箱
24. emergency[ɪˈmɜːdʒənsɪ] _____ n. 突发事件,紧急状态
25. touch-up kit _____ 补妆包
26. sewing kit _____ 针线包
27. grooming[ˈgruːmɪŋ] _____ n. 打扮,装束
28. toiletry[ˈtɔɪlətrɪ] _____ n. 洗漱用品
29. domestic[dəˈmestɪk] _____ adj. 国内的,家庭的
30. category[ˈkætəgərɪ] _____ n. 类别
31. dominate[ˈdɒmɪneɪt] _____ v. 支配,控制,(在比赛中)占有优势,占据主动

32. approximately[əˈprɒksɪmətlɪ] _____ adv. 大约,大概
33. innovation[ˌɪnəˈveɪʃn] _____ n. 改革,创新
34. characteristic[ˌkærəktəˈrɪstɪk] _____ n. 特点,特征,品质
35. surpass[səˈpɑːs] _____ v. 超过,超越
36. Asia-Pacific _____ 亚太地区
37. be concerned about _____ 关注
38. account for _____ (数量或比例上)占,导致

Unit 6

1. appointment[əˈpɔɪntmənt] _____ n. 约会,预约,约定
2. book[bʊk] _____ v. 预订,预约
3. vacancy[ˈveɪkənsɪ] _____ n. 空处,空位
4. schedule[ˈskedʒuːl] _____ v. 为……安排时间,安排,排定
5. time slot _____ 时段
6. in case _____ 以防万一
7. glitter[ˈglɪtə(r)] _____ n. 闪烁,闪耀,闪光
8. file[faɪl] _____ v. 锉平,锉光滑,锉去
9. cuticle[ˈkjuːtɪkl] _____ n. (指甲或趾甲根部的)角质层
10. nourished[ˈnʌrɪʃt] _____ adj. 滋养的
11. floral[ˈflɔːrəl] _____ adj. 用花制作的,饰以花卉图案的
12. option[ˈɒpʃn] _____ n. 选择,选项,选择权
13. seal[siːl] _____ v. 封,密封
14. glossy[ˈglɒsɪ] _____ adj. 平滑有光泽的
15. nail polish _____ 指甲油
16. a hint of _____ 一丝
17. on the tip _____ 在尖端
18. surge[sɜːdʒ] _____ n. 陡增,剧增,急剧上升
19. flourishing[ˈflʌrɪʃɪŋ] _____ adj. 茁壮成长的,繁荣的,蓬勃发展的
20. evolve[ɪˈvɒlv] _____ v. (使)逐步发展,(使)逐渐形成
21. pedicure[ˈpedɪkjʊə(r)] _____ n. 美足,足部保养
22. prompt[prɒmpt] _____ v. 引起,导致,激起
23. diversification[daɪˌvɜːsɪfɪˈkeɪʃn] _____ n. 多样化
24. showcase[ˈʃəʊkeɪs] _____ v. 展示……的优点,充分展示
25. durability[ˌdjʊərəˈbɪlətɪ] _____ n. 耐用性,持久性

26. venture [ˈventʃə(r)]   n.（有风险的）企业，投机活动，商业冒险
27. acumen [ˈækjəmən]   n. 敏锐，精明
28. opt for   选择
29. gel and acrylic nail extensions   凝胶和丙烯酸延伸甲

Unit 7

1. regulation [ˌregjuˈleɪʃn]   n. 规章制度，规则
2. provision [prəˈvɪʒn]   n. 条款，规定
3. promulgate [ˈprɒmlgeɪt]   v. 发布，颁布（新法律）
4. supervision [ˌsuːpəˈvɪʒn]   n. 监督，管理
5. implement [ˈɪmplɪmənt]   v. 执行，贯彻
6. registration [ˌredʒɪˈstreɪʃn]   n. 登记，注册
7. registrant [ˈredʒɪstrənt]   n. 注册人
8. be responsible for   对……负责
9. record-filing management   备案管理
10. recordation entity   备案人
11. consist of   由……组成
12. Party Central Committee   党中央
13. State Council   国务院
14. legislation [ˌledʒɪsˈleɪʃn]   n. 立法，制定法律
15. enforcement [ɪnˈfɔːsmənt]   n. 执行，实施
16. indication [ˌɪndɪˈkeɪʃn]   n. 适应证
17. contraindication [ˌkɒntrəˌɪndɪˈkeɪʃn]   n. 禁忌证
18. precaution [prɪˈkɔːʃn]   n. 注意事项，预防措施
19. guardian [ˈɡɑːdɪən]   n. 监护人
20. qualification [ˌkwɒlɪfɪˈkeɪʃn]   n. 资格，学历
21. device [dɪˈvaɪs]   n. 设备，装置
22. Ministry of Health   卫生部
23. National Administration of Traditional Chinese Medicine   国家中医药管理局
24. medical risk   医疗风险
25. graded management   分级管理

Unit 8

1. pimple['pɪmpl] n. 痤疮,粉刺
2. sebum['siːbəm] n. 皮脂
3. secretion[sɪ'kriːʃn] n. 分泌,分泌物
4. pore[pɔː] n. (皮肤上的)毛孔,(植物的)气孔,孔隙
5. scar[skɑː] n. 瘢痕,伤痕
6. mask[mɑːsk] n. 面膜,面罩
7. serum['sɪərəm] n. 精华素,乳清,血清
8. toner['təʊnə] n. 爽肤水,墨粉
9. herbal['hɜːbl] adj. 药草的 n. 草本植物志
10. regeneration[rɪˌdʒenə'reɪʃn] n. 再生,重生
11. metabolism[mə'tæbəlɪzəm] n. 新陈代谢
12. inflammation[ˌɪnflə'meɪʃn] n. 炎症,发炎
13. crop up 出现,发生
14. take effect 产生效果
15. verbal['vɜːbl] adj. 语言的,文字的
16. understanding[ˌʌndə'stændɪŋ] n. 理解,了解,谅解
17. interpersonal[ˌɪntə'pɜːsənl] adj. 人际的,人际关系的
18. consultation[ˌkɒnsl'teɪʃn] n. 咨询,商讨
19. expectation[ˌekspek'teɪʃn] n. 预期,期望
20. moderate['mɒdərət] adj. 适度的,适中的,温和的
21. preference['prefrəns] n. 偏爱,喜爱,偏爱的事物
22. terminology[ˌtɜːmɪ'nɒlədʒɪ] n. (某学科的)术语,专门用语
23. precise[prɪ'saɪs] adj. 精确的,准确的,确切的
24. dissatisfied[dɪs'sætɪsfaɪd] adj. (对……)不满的,不满意的
25. tactfully['tæktfəlɪ] adv. 巧妙地,言行得体地
26. non-verbal[nɒn'vɜːbl] adj. 非语言的
27. beautician[bjuː'tɪʃn] n. 美容师
28. intangible[ɪn'tændʒəbl] adj. 无形的
29. constitute['kɒnstɪtjuːt] v. 组成,构成
30. posture['pɒstʃə(r)] n. (坐,立的)姿势,态度,立场
31. gesture['dʒestʃə(r)] n. 手势,示意动作
32. squat[skwɒt] v. 蹲

33. etiquette['etɪket] _____ n. 礼节,礼仪,规矩
34. facial['feɪʃl] _____ adj. 面部的
35. familiarity[fə͵mɪlɪ'ærətɪ] _____ n. 亲近,友好随和
36. rigid['rɪdʒɪd] _____ adj. 僵硬的,死板的,固执的
37. beauty salon _____ 美容院

Appendix B Common Cosmetic Brands
附录 B 常见美容产品品牌名称

China 中国

羽西	Yue Sai
花西子	Florasis
百雀羚	Pechoin
高夫	gf
佰草集	Herborist
薇诺娜	Winona
珀莱雅	Proya
颐莲	Rellet
完美日记	Perfect Diary
心慕与你	Into You
橘朵	Judydoll
卡姿兰	Carslan
花洛莉亚	Flortte
珂拉琪	Colorkey
稚优泉	Chioture
酵色	Joocyee
毛戈平	MAOGEPING
自然堂	Chando
欧诗漫	OSM
一叶子	One Leaf
相宜本草	Inoherb
丸美	Marubi
魔法世家	Mask Family
美加净	Maxam
玛丽黛佳	Marie Dalgar

雅邦	Alobon
火烈鸟	Flamingo
戈戈舞	Gogotales
植物医生	Dr Plant
韩束	Kans
半亩花田	Little Dream Garden
玉泽	Dr. Yu
丁家宜	Tjoy
花知晓	Flower Knows
溪木源	Simpcare
冰希黎	Boitown
姗拉娜	Sunrana
润百颜	Biohyalux
美肤宝	MEIFUBAO
嘉利玛	Galimard
滋色	Zeesea
悠宜	Unny Club
高姿	COGI
温碧泉	Wetherm
阿芙	AFU
森田药妆	Dr. Morita
舞动奇迹	Dancing Up
如薇	RNW
雪玲妃	Snefe
韩佳妮	KanJN
毕生之研	Peterson's Lab
水密码	Wetcode

France 法国

Chanel	香奈儿
Dior	迪奥
L'Oreal	欧莱雅
Helena Rubinstein	赫莲娜
YSL	圣罗兰

Givenchy	纪梵希
Lancôme	兰蔻
Guerlain	娇兰
Bourjois	妙巴黎
Chantecaille	香缇卡
Make Up For Ever	玫珂菲
Vichy	薇姿
Fresh	馥蕾诗
Clarins	娇韵诗
Avène	雅漾
Evian	依云
Sisley	希思黎
Payot	柏姿
Bioderma	贝德玛
Cetaphil	丝塔芙

USA 美国

MAC	魅可
Maybelline	美宝莲
Tom Ford	汤姆福特
Avon	雅芳
Benefit	贝玲妃
Bobbi Brown	芭比波朗
Elizabeth Arden	伊丽莎白·雅顿
Nars	纳斯(娜斯)
Anna Sui	安娜苏
Max Factor	蜜丝佛陀
Estée Lauder	雅诗兰黛
Mary Kay	玫琳凯
Olay	玉兰油
Clinique	倩碧
Pond's	旁氏
Johnson & Johnson	强生
Neutrogena	露得清

Revlon	露华浓
Origins	悦木之源
Mentholatum	曼秀雷敦
La Mer	海蓝之谜
Artistry	雅姿
Clean & Clear	可伶可俐
Blistex	碧唇
Kiehl's	科颜氏

Italy 意大利

Gucci	古驰
Armani	阿玛尼
Kiko	奇蔻
Diego Dalla Palma	迪亚哥帕玛
Borghese	贝佳斯
Pupa	宝柏
Nina Ricci	莲娜丽姿
Collistar	蔻意诗

Korea 韩国

Sulwhasoo	雪花秀
Whoo	后
Etude House	伊蒂之屋
Clio	珂莱欧
It's Skin	伊思
Aekyung	爱敬
Luna	露娜
Laneige	兰芝
Tfit	媞妃特
Babrea	芭贝拉
Dr. Jart+	蒂佳婷

Innisfree	悦诗风吟
Hera	赫拉
Mamonde	梦妆
O HUI	欧惠
The Face Shop	菲诗小铺
3CE	三熹玉
IOPE	亦博（艾诺碧）
Too Cool for School	涂酷
Skin Food	思亲肤
Mediheal	美迪惠尔
The Saem	得鲜
Romand	柔魅得
Cell Fusion C	秀肤生
Missha	谜尚
Charmzone	婵真
Nature Republic	自然乐园
JMsolution	肌司妍
Banila CO	芭妮兰
Papa Recipe	春雨

Japan 日本

Kosé	高丝
Suqqu	苏酷
Kanebo	佳丽宝
Freeplus	芙丽芳丝
Bioré	碧柔
Kate	凯朵
Pola	宝丽
Jurlique	茱莉蔻
CPB	肌肤之钥
Shiseido	资生堂
Anessa	安耐晒（安热沙）
Benefique	碧丽妃
Aupres	欧珀莱

Za	姬芮
Pure & Mild	泊美
Shu Uemura	植村秀
Canmake	井田
DHC	蝶翠诗
Cosme Decorte	黛珂
Kiss Me	奇士美
SK-II	美之匙
Dr. Ci:Labo	城野医生
Opera	娥佩兰
Naris	娜丽丝
Sekkisei	雪肌精

References 参考文献

[1] 曹立娅,李远.中医英语视听说[M].青岛:中国海洋大学出版社,2014.

[2] 冯居秦,杨国峰,张伟明.中医美容英语[M].武汉:华中科技大学出版社,2019.

[3] 李思彦.化妆品专业英语[M].北京:化学工业出版社,2020.

[4] 廖温魁.韩非子(大中华文库)(汉英对照)[M].北京:商务印书馆,2015.

[5] 刘建军.工匠精神及其当代价值[J].思想教育研究,2016(10):36-40,85.

[6] 施建蓉,周恩.中医英语[M].3版.上海:上海科学技术出版社,2020.

[7] 王小寒,余香庆.2022年度"最美巴渝工匠"巡礼④丨李真芹:技能"妆"办人生,匠心为美赋能[N/OL].重庆日报,2022-12-15.https://wap.cqrb.cn/xcq/NewsDetail?classId=134&classId=134&newsId=1323542&id=1323542.

[8] 许先本.美容服务与策划(上)[M].北京:北京师范大学出版社,2013.

[9] 张卫华,余芊芊.实用美容英语会话[M].武汉:华中科技大学出版社,2017.

[10] Barel A O, Paye M, Maibach H I. Handbook of cosmetic science and technology[M]. Boca Raton:Taylor & Francis Group,2014.

[11] Grama G. The 25 best makeup brands in 2023[EB/OL].(2023-05-12). https://luxatic.com/best-makeup-brands/.

[12] Margaret H, Jones E. Massage for therapists:a guide to soft tissue therapy [M]. 3rd ed. New Jersey:Wiley-Blackwell,2009.

[13] Turner L H, West R. An introduction to communication[M]. Cambridge: Cambridge University Press,2018.

[14] Ma Y H. Cosmetics market in China-statistics & facts[EB/OL].(2023-07-03). https://www.statista.com/topics/1897/cosmetics-in-china/#topicOverview (August 1,2023).

参 考 网 址

[1]　https://www.dhgate.com/product/7-colors-led-facial-face-mask-machine-photon/487806867.html

[2]　https://www.statista.com/topics/1897/cosmetics-in-china/#topicOverview

声明：

1. 本教材所参考法律法规均来自官方网站，在此未单独做出标注。

2. 本教材编写过程中使用了部分图片，在此向这些图片的版权所有人表示诚挚的谢意！由于客观原因，我们无法联系到您，请相关版权所有人与出版社联系，出版社将按照国家相关规定和行业标准支付稿酬。

3. 感谢廊坊职业技术学院李健老师朗读 Unit 1 中的 *The Reed*。此外，音、视频仅作为本教材配套资源教学使用，未经允许，请勿作其他用途。